THE YEAR YO WERE BORN
1972

CW00584675

A fascinating book about the year 1972 with information on:
Events of the year UK, Adverts of 1972, Cost of living, Births, Sporting events,
Book publications, Movies, Music, World events and People in power.

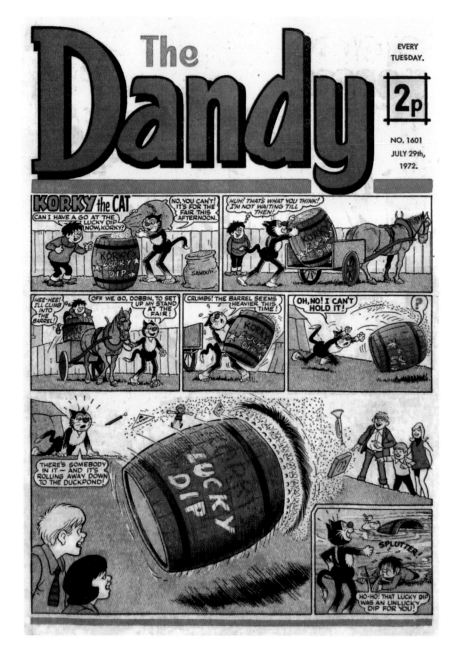

INDEX

UK EVENTS OF 1972

January

1st | Welsh rugby captain John Dawes is made an OBE in the New Year Honours List.

2nd | Dame Rose Heilbron DBE was a High Court judge, previously a barrister of the post-war period in the United Kingdom. Her career included many "firsts" for a woman – she was the first woman to achieve a first class honours degree in law at the University of Liverpool the first woman to win a scholarship to Gray's Inn, one of the first two women to be appointed King's Counsel in England, the first woman to lead in a murder case, the first woman recorder, the first woman judge to sit at the Old Bailey, and the first woman treasurer of Gray's Inn. She was also the second woman to be appointed a High Court judge, after Elizabeth Lane.

9th | The National Union of Mineworkers held a strike ballot in which 58.8% voted in favour of industrial action. Coal miners begin a strike which lasts for seven weeks, including picketing of Saltley coke depot in Birmingham.

17th | The "West Belfast Seven" Provisional Irish Republican Army (IRA) internees escape from prison ship Maidstone moored in Belfast Lough by swimming ashore.

19th | The government announces the lifting of all restrictions on broadcasting hours on television and radio.

20th | The premiere of Pink Floyd's The Dark Side of the Moon at The Dome, Brighton, is halted by technical difficulties. The Dark Side of the Moon would be played in its entirety the following night, but it would be a full year before the album was released.

21st | Keith Richards jumps on stage to jam with Chuck Berry at the Hollywood Palladium, but is ordered off for playing too loud. Berry later claims that he did not recognize Keith and would not have booted him if he did.

January

22nd Unemployment exceeded the 1,000,000 mark for the first time since the 1930s - almost double the 582,000 who were unemployed when Edward Heath's Conservative government came to power less than two years ago.

30th Bloody Sunday, or the Bogside Massacre, was a massacre on 30 January 1972 in the Bogside area of Derry, Northern Ireland, when British soldiers shot 26 civilians during a protest march against internment without trial. Fourteen people died: 13 were killed outright, while the death of another man four months later was attributed to his injuries. Many of the victims were shot while fleeing from the soldiers, and some were shot while trying to help the wounded. Other protesters were injured by shrapnel, rubber bullets, or batons, and two were run down by army vehicles. All of those shot were Catholics. The march had been organised by the Northern Ireland Civil Rights Association. The soldiers were from the 1st Battalion, Parachute Regiment, the same regiment implicated in the Ballymurphy massacre several months prior.

February

2nd On the day that funerals were held for victims of Bloody Sunday in Londonderry, a huge mob destroyed the British Embassy in Dublin. Over the preceding three days rioting had got steadily worse, and the Embassy had already been evacuated by diplomats and other staff members, only a few guards remaining to defend the building.

3rd The Start of the winter Olympic Games. Great Britain and Northern Ireland competed at the Winter Olympics in Sapporo, Japan, but did not win any medals.

5th 91 people are hurt and 122 arrested as mounted police charge protestors in London.

9th Paul McCartney's new band, Wings, make their live debut at the University of Nottingham. It is McCartney's first public concert since The Beatles' 1966 US tour.

A state of emergency was declared by Heath as a result of the miners' strike.

12th The United Kingdom held a national preselection to choose the song that would go to the Eurovision Song Contest 1972. It was held on 12th February 1972 and presented by Cliff Richard as a special edition of his BBC1 TV series It's Cliff Richard! All songs were performed by the group The New Seekers, the first group ever to represent the UK in the contest and the first quintet ever to appear in Eurovision as a group.

13th Led Zeppelin's concert in Singapore is cancelled when government officials will not let them off the airplane because of their long hair.

19th Paul McCartney's single "Give Ireland Back to the Irish" (which was inspired by the "Bloody Sunday" massacre in Ireland on 30 January 1972) is banned by the BBC.

22nd An Official Irish Republican Army bomb killed six people in the Aldershot Barracks bombing.

28th The 1972 UK miners' strike was a major dispute over pay between the National Union of Mineworkers (NUM) and the Conservative Edward Heath government of the United Kingdom. Miners' wages had not kept pace with those of other industrial workers since 1960. The strike began on 9th January 1972 and ended on 28th February 1972.

March

1st Border begins broadcasting in colour from the Selkirk transmitter.

Ford announced its new Granada model, available as a saloon, coupé or estate car, which would be built at the Dagenham plant in England as well as the Cologne plant in West Germany. It was designed to compete with the likes of the Rover P6 and Vauxhall Victor, and would be sold as the Ford Consul in mainland Europe.

4th The 1972 Football League Cup Final took place on 4th March 1972 at Wembley Stadium and was contested by Chelsea and Stoke City. Chelsea went into the match as strong favourites having won the FA Cup and the UEFA Cup Winners' Cup in the previous two seasons, whereas Stoke were attempting to win their first major trophy. Terry Conroy put Stoke into the lead early on but Chelsea hit back through Peter Osgood just before half time. Stoke got the decisive final goal from veteran George Eastham to end their 109-year wait for a major honour. It remains the club's only major trophy victory; the closest they have come since then to beating this achievement was in 2011 when they lost to Manchester City in the 2011 FA Cup Final.

The 1972 Women's Open Squash Championships was held at the BP Club in Lower Sydenham, London from 4th –9th March 1972.Heather McKay won her eleventh consecutive title defeating Kathy Malan in the final. This surpassed the previous record of ten wins set by Janet Morgan from 1950 through to 1959.

6th As a result of the Beeching cuts, the line beyond Keswick to Cockermouth and Workington was closed on 18 April 1966, leaving a single line branch between Keswick and Penrith. The station survived for six years before closing on 6 March 1972.

15th Two British soldiers killed when attempting to defuse a bomb in Belfast; an RUC officer is also killed in an IRA attack in Coalisland, County Tyrone.

21st Chancellor Anthony Barber announced a £1,200,000,000 tax reduction in the Budget.

25th The 17th Eurovision Song Contest is held at the Usher Hall in Edinburgh. Luxembourg wins the contest with the song "Après toi", performed by Vicky Leandros. The UK went on to finish second with 114pts.

26th The UK's last trolleybus system, in Bradford, was closed.

31st A CND demonstration was held protesting against the nuclear base at Aldermaston.

April

1st | William Whitelaw was appointed as the first Northern Ireland Secretary.

2nd | First edition of the comedy panel game I'm Sorry I Haven't a Clue is aired on BBC Radio 4. In 2020 (when it will still be running) the programme will be voted the greatest radio comedy of all time by a panel convened by Radio Times.

3rd | Terry Wogan joins Radio 2 to present the new weekday breakfast show.

4th | After a three-year courtship, Emily Nugent marries Ernest Bishop on Coronation Street.

 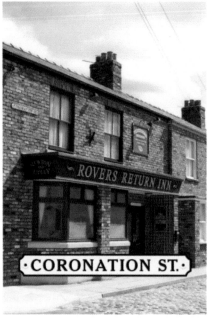

6th | Ford launches a new flagship saloon model, the Granada, which replaces the Zephyr on the UK market and will be produced at the Dagenham plant as well as Ford's Cologne plant in West Germany.

11th | The BBC Radio 4 parodic panel show I'm Sorry I Haven't a Clue was broadcast for the first time.

14th | The Provisional Irish Republican Army explodes twenty-four bombs in towns and cities across Northern Ireland.

16th | Electric Light Orchestra make their live debut at the Fox and Greyhound pub in Park Lane, Croydon, England.

19th | British Prime Minister Edward Heath confirms that a plan to conduct an arrest operation, in the event of a riot during the march on 30th January 1972, was known to British government Ministers in advance.

22nd | An 11-year-old boy killed by a rubber bullet fired by the British Army in Belfast; he was the first to die from a rubber bullet impact.

23rd | The Sunday Times Insight Team publish their account of the events of 'Bloody Sunday'.

May

2nd Stone the Crows lead guitarist Les Harvey is electrocuted on stage during a show in Swansea, Wales, by touching a poorly connected microphone. Harvey died in a hospital a few hours later. The band's lead singer, Maggie Bell, Harvey's long-time girlfriend, was also hospitalized, having collapsed on stage after the incident.

3rd In the first UEFA Cup final, Tottenham Hotspur beat Wolverhampton Wanderers 2–1 in the first leg at the Molineux.

6th Leeds United won the FA Cup for the first time with a 1–0 win over last year's winners Arsenal at Wembley Stadium. The only goal is a header by Allan Clarke from a Mick Jones pass.

12th Crown Court established by the Courts Act 1971 to replace the courts of Assize and Quarter Sessions in England and Wales. Property qualifications requiring jurors to be householders are abolished.

17th Tottenham Hotspur completed a 3-2 aggregate win over Wolverhampton Wanderers at White Hart Lane to win the first UEFA Cup.

18th Queen Elizabeth II met her uncle, Edward, Duke of Windsor for the last time, at his home in Paris.

Four troopers of the Special Air Service and Special Boat Service were parachuted onto the ocean liner Queen Elizabeth 2 1,000 miles (1,600 km) across the Atlantic after a bomb threat and a ransom demand which turned out to be bogus.

24th The final stretch of the M6 motorway opened between junctions 6 (Spaghetti Junction) and 7 north of Birmingham, with the fully operational motorway stretching more than 200 miles from Rugby to Carlisle, more than a decade after the first sections were opened.

June

1st | Hotels and boarding houses became required to obtain certification under the Fire Precautions Act 1971.

2nd | Two British soldiers die in an IRA land mine attack near Rosslea, County Fermanagh.

5th | The funeral of The Duke of Windsor (formerly King Edward VIII) is held at Windsor Castle.

6th | David Bowie releases his breakthrough album "The Rise & Fall of Ziggy Stardust and the Spiders from Mars".

12th | John Lennon's political album "Sometime in NYC" released including the songs "Woman is the Nigger of the World", "Attica State" and "Luck of the Irish".

14th | Members of the NI Social Democratic and Labour Party hold a meeting with representatives of the Irish Republican Army in Derry; the IRA representatives outline their conditions for talks with the British Government.

18th | British European Airways Flight 548 crashed near Staines and 118 people are killed, making it the UK's worst air disaster at this date. The only two survivors both die by the time they reach a hospital.

19th | Hundreds of thousands of holidaymakers face flight delays and cancellations after pilots threaten to strike over hijack fears.

20th | Secret Meeting Between IRA and British Officials held.

22nd | The Irish Republican Army announced that it would call a ceasefire from 26th June 1972 provided that there is a "reciprocal response" from the security forces.

23rd | The Chancellor of the Exchequer Anthony Barber announced a decision to float the Pound.

26th | The Provisional Irish Republican Army (IRA) killed two British Army soldiers in separate attacks during the day and at midnight begins a "bi-lateral truce".

July

1st | The first official gay pride march in London was held.

7th | Secret Talks Between IRA and British Government: Gerry Adams is part of a delegation to London for talks with the British Government.

8th | Granada broadcasts Sesame Street for the first time.

9th | Springhill Massacre: British snipers shoot dead five Catholic civilians and wounded two others in Springhill, Belfast. The ceasefire between the Provisional IRA and the British Army comes to an end.

12th | Following the enabling of The Sound Broadcasting Act 1972, The Independent Broadcasting Authority is formed, paving the way for the launch of Independent Local Radio.

15th | "Honky Chateau" becomes Elton John's first No. 1 album in the US, includes hit "Rocket Man".

18th | Leader of the British Labour Party Harold Wilson holds meeting with representatives of the Irish Republican Army.

21st | Bloody Friday: within the space of seventy-five minutes, the Provisional Irish Republican Army explode twenty-two bombs in Belfast; six civilians, two British Army soldiers and one UDA volunteer were killed, 130 injured.

28th | A strike by thousands of dockers led to the government announcing a state of emergency on 4th August.

31st | Operation Motorman was a large operation carried out by the British Army (HQ Northern Ireland) in Northern Ireland during the Troubles. The operation took place in the early hours of 31 July 1972 with the aim of retaking the "no-go areas" (areas controlled by residents, including Irish republican paramilitaries) that had been established in Belfast and other urban centres. In Derry, Operation Carcan, initially proposed as a separate operation, was executed as part of Motorman.

August

3rd | British premier Edward Heath proclaims emergency crisis due to dock strike.

5th | The group Moody Blues release "Nights in White Satin".

6th | Idi Amin, dictator of Uganda, announced that 50,000 Asians with British passports are to be expelled from Uganda to the United Kingdom within the next three months as they are "sabotaging the Ugandan economy".

9th | The Tim Rice and Andrew Lloyd Webber musical Jesus Christ Superstar made its West End debut.

10th | Paul & Linda McCartney are arrested in Sweden on drug possession.

11th | Two IRA members are killed when a bomb they were transporting exploded prematurely.

21st | British dock strike ends after dockers accept an amended Jones-Adlington Agreement.

22nd | IRA bomb explodes prematurely at a customs post at Newry, County Down - 9 people, including three members of the IRA and five Catholic civilians are killed in the explosion.

26th | Great Britain and Northern Ireland competed at the Olympics in Munich, West Germany, and win 4 gold 5 silver and 9 bronze medals.

28th | Prince William of Gloucester, a cousin of the Queen, is killed in an air crash near Wolverhampton. He was thirty years old, a bachelor and ninth-in-line to the British throne at the time.

30th | John Lennon and Yoko Ono's "One on One" benefit shows (matinee and evening) for children at Madison Square Garden, New York, his final full concert performance.

September

1st | Rising of school leaving age in England and Wales from fifteen to sixteen for pupils leaving school at the end of the academic year began. Many temporary new buildings were erected in secondary modern and comprehensive schools to accommodate the older pupils, while some authorities rose the secondary school transfer age from 11 to 12 or 13. The age was also raised in Scotland and Northern Ireland.

2nd | Rod Stewart's 1st #1 hit (You Wear it Well).

3rd | Great Britain's Mary Peters sets a new world record of 4801 points to win the Munich Olympics pentathlon gold by just 10 points from Heide Rosendahl of West Germany.

10th | 3 British soldiers are killed in a land mine attack near Dungannon, County Tyrone.

11th | The BBC1 television quiz programme Mastermind was broadcast for the first time.

12th | The sinking of two British trawlers by an Icelandic gunboat triggered the second Cod War.

September

13th Hypermarkets make their debut in the United Kingdom some twenty years after their debut in France, when French retail giant Carrefour opens a hypermarket in Caerphilly, South Wales.

18th Thousands of Ugandan Asians arrived in the UK after being deported by Idi Amin.

19th A parcel bomb sent to Israeli Embassy in London kills one diplomat.

20th Police find cannabis growing on Paul & Linda McCartney's farm.

The Social Democratic and Labour Party issues a document entitled "Towards a New Ireland", proposing that the British and Irish governments should have joint sovereignty over Northern Ireland.

28th David Bowie sells out his 1st show in NY Carnegie Hall.

October

1st London Weekend Television launches the UK's first Sunday politics programme – Weekend World. It continues until 1988.

2nd Following the lifting of restrictions on broadcasting hours, BBC1 and ITV are allowed to begin broadcasting during the day. BBC1's afternoon schedule launches with the first edition of a new lunchtime magazine programme Pebble Mill at One.

8th David Hughes is taken ill while singing the role of Pinkerton in Madam Butterfly in London. He completes the performance but dies shortly afterwards of heart failure.

10th John Betjeman was appointed Poet Laureate.

13th Bank rates were abolished and replaced with the Minimum Lending Rate.

16th The first episode of Emmerdale Farm, a soap opera set in rural Yorkshire, was broadcast on ITV.

19th Royce Ryton's play about the Abdication Crisis of Edward VIII, Crown Matrimonial, premiered at the Theatre Royal, Haymarket, London, for the first time includes the portrayal of a living member of the Royal Family (Queen Elizabeth The Queen Mother as The Duchess of York) on the legitimate stage.

October

22nd | Gordon Banks, the England national football team goalkeeper, suffered a serious eye injury in a car crash in Staffordshire.

23rd | Access credit cards were introduced.

24th | 2 Catholic men are found dead at a farm at Aughinahinch, near Newtownbbutler, County Fermanagh - British soldiers carry out the killings.

30th | The Northern Ireland Office issues a discussion document 'The Future of Northern Ireland'; the paper states Britain's commitment to the union as long as the majority of people wish to remain part of the United Kingdom.

November

4th | Radios 2 and 4 begin broadcasting in stereo in South East England. Stereo is rolled out to the rest of the country over subsequent years.

6th | The Government introduces price and pay freezes to counter inflation.

11th | Rugby League World Cup, Stade de Gerland, Lyon, France: Australia and Great Britain draw 10-10; Great Britain awarded the Trophy.

16th | British Prime Minister Edward Heath warns against a Unilateral Declaration of Independence.

18th | England women's national football team played its first official association football match, against Scotland in Greenock, 100 years after the equivalent men's match.

19th | Formation in Coventry of the PEOPLE Party, predecessor of the Green Party and the first political party in Europe to promote Green politics.

22nd | 2 British soldiers are killed in a booby trap bomb in Cullyhanna, County Armagh.

26th | Bomb explosion at the Film Centre Cinema, in O'Connell Bridge House in Dublin.

December

1st | 2 people killed and 127 injured when 2 car bombs explode in the centre of Dublin, Republic of Ireland.

10th | John Hicks was awarded the Nobel Prize in Economics with Kenneth Arrow for "pioneering contributions to general economic equilibrium theory and welfare theory."

Rodney Robert Porter won the Nobel Prize in Physiology or Medicine jointly with Gerald Edelman "for their discoveries concerning the chemical structure of antibodies".

30th | The BBC airs part one of "The Three Doctors", a four-part serial of the science-fiction programme Doctor Who created to celebrate its tenth series (the tenth anniversary will not be until 23rd November of the following year).

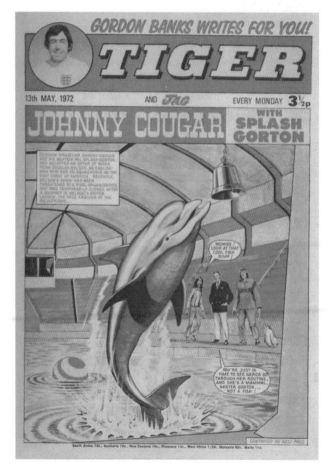

IRELANDS Nº1 MAGAZINE STORY BOOK FOR BOYS

OUR BOYS

DECEMBER **1972**
price **10 pence**

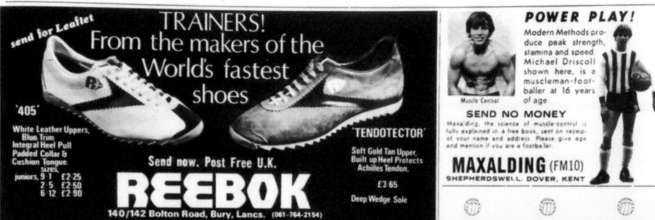

16

To a man they say Cutty Sark.

And when it comes to Scotch, Cutty Sark says it all.

Cutty Sark Scots Whisky. The only one of its kind.

Löwenbräu costs more than beer.

May the Holidays bring you

Johnnie Walker Red

SIP INTO SOMETHING COMFORTABLE

You know how it is when you've been on the go.
You want to relax. And so does he.
To put up his feet and put down a Guinness.
It's a great comfort after a hard day. So nice to come
home to (so make sure there's some in the house).

There's more than goodness in Guinness

MARATHON BRED—RALLY TESTED
that's the heart of today's best value in '1500s'

The Moskvich engine is a real 90 mph. plus, rally winner! It's the same standard 1,478 cc., all alloy, overhead camshaft engine that so successfully powered the team of three Moskvich saloons which finished the gruelling, 16,000 mile World Cup Rally – as well as the earlier London to Sydney Marathon success.

Both the Moskvich '1500' saloon and estate are smart, comfortable models with up-to-the-minute styling. They come in a choice of bright modern colours, too.

At the amazingly low prices of £692.73* for the saloon, and £772.48* for the estate – you buy in-built Moskvich reliability. Reliability bred from the Steppes of Russia to the rally winner's rostrum!

And you also buy a list of standard features that most other manufacturers only fit as extras! Fully reclining seats, ammeter, oil pressure gauge, cigarette lighter, reversing lamps, armrests on all doors, two-speed wipers, radiator blind, underbonnet inspection lamp, a 22-piece tool kit – and more besides!

That's value for money . . . *and* they're built to last.

1478cc 90mph £692.73*

*Recommended price delivery ex-Byfleet.

1478cc 90mph £772.48*

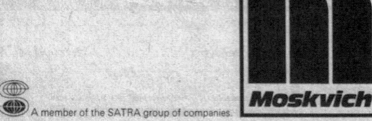

Moskvich

For a copy of our detailed colour literature on the Moskvich range see your nearest dealer on the list printed opposite.

A member of the SATRA group of companies.

Satra Motors Ltd., Sole U.K. Moskvich Concessionaires, Canada Road, Oyster Lane, Byfleet, Surrey. Tel: Byfleet 44221

"VALLEY OF FLAME"-NEW PICTURE STORY INSIDE!

June

APRIL 22nd 1972

EVERY TUESDAY

SHE DANCES WHILE HER HEART IS BREAKING...
See MY NAME IS NOBODY, the touching story of two wartime orphans

Ark Concert Presentations Present-
Rock At The Oval 1972

FRANK ZAPPA
HAWKWIND
MAN
LINDA LEWIS
BIGGLES
SAM APPLE PIE

SPECIAL GUESTS: **JEFF BECK GROUP**

SAT.16.SEPT. TICKETS £2·00
MIDDAY-9PM

From All Branches Of Harlequin Record Shops
The Oval

& One Stop Records 97 Dean St W1
40 South Molton St W1
2 The Square Richmond

TICKETS BY POST FROM HARLEQUIN RECORDS
67 GT TITCHFIELD ST LONDON W1

Be smart this season. Be your size.

There's a true and proper size for you to be. Any more and you have to go up a size to get a dress that won't feel like a body stocking on you.

So be the size you're meant to be. Watch your weight, cut down on Calories.

For instance, where you'd use a teaspoonful of sugar, use one tiny, sensible Sweetex instead.

It's just as sweet as sugar. But, where a teaspoonful of sugar has 27 Calories, Sweetex has none.

If you can avoid 27 Calories every time you have a cup of tea or coffee, it's a help.

The 500 tube of Sweetex saves you adding 13,500 Calories to your dress-buying problems.

A sweet thought.

SWEETEX

Smarter than Calories.

Clothes by Deliss, Boston 151, Herbert Johnson.
Weight watching by Sweetex.

COST OF LIVING 1972

A conversion of pre-decimal to decimal money

The Pound, 1971 became the year of decimalization when the pound became 100 new pennies. Prior to that the pound was equivalent to 20 shillings. Money prior to 1971 was written £/s/d. (d being for pence). Below is a chart explaining the monetary value of each coin before and after 1971.

Symbol	Before 1971	After 1971
£	Pound (240 pennies)	Pound (100 new pennies)
s	Shilling (12 pennies)	5 pence
d	Penny	¼ of a penny
¼d	Farthing	1 penny
½d	Halfpenny	½ pence
3d	Threepence	About 1/80 of a pound
4d	Groat (four pennies)	
6d	Sixpence (Tanner)	2½ new pence
2s	Florin (2 shillings)	10 pence
2s/6d	Half a crown (2 shillings and 6 pence)	12½ pence
5s	Crown	25 pence
10s	10 shilling note (10 bob)	50 pence
10s/6d	½ Guinea	52½ pence
21s	1 Guinea	105 pence

Prices are in equivalent to new pence today and on average throughout the UK.

Item	1972	Price equivalent today
Wages, average yearly	£1,351.00	£17,293.00
Average house price	£6,008.00	£76,902.00
Price of an average car	£1,240.00	£15,872.00
Litre of petrol	£0.08p	99p
Flour 1.5kg	£0.13p	£1.66p
Bread (loaf)	£0.10p	£1.28p
Sugar 1kg	£0.10p	£1.28p
Milk 1 pint	£0.20p	£2.56p
Butter 250g	£0.12p	£1.57p
Cheese 400g	£0.28p	£3.53p
Potatoes 2.5kg	£0.13p	£1.60p
Bacon 400g	£0.48p	£6.09p

Beer prices reported July 1972

Product	Percentage alcohol	Pence per pint
Youngers IPA	4.6	13 -13.5
Bass Charrington IPA Best	3.8	14-17
Courage Best Bitter	4.1	13
Ind Coope Best Bitter	3.4	13
Watney `Special'	3.4	12.5
Whitbread Trophy	3.7	13
Adnams Best Bitter	3.5	12
Batham	3.5	12
Devenish	2.7	12-13
Greenhall Whitley	3.9	13
Greene King IPA	3.7	13
Hall Woodhouse Badger Best	4.0	13
Jennings Castle	3.7	12
Theakstons Best	3.6	13
Trumans Special	3.9	15
Vaux - Sampson	3.9	13
Youngs	3.5	13

On the 26th November 2008, trading of shares in Woolworths Group was suspended, and its Woolworths and Entertainment UK subsidiaries entered administration. Deloitte closed all 807 Woolworth's stores between the 27th December 2008 and the 6th January 2009, resulting in 27,000 job losses. Woolworths Group plc entered administration on 27th January 2009, and it was officially dissolved on the 13th October 2015.

In February 2009, Shop Direct Group purchased the Woolworths trademark and internet address, which continued as a retail website until its closure in June 2015. As of April 2017, after former director Tony Page expressed a wish to buy the Woolworths name from Shop Direct, there was talk of Woolworths making a comeback to British high streets.

Wynne Evans, MStJ, was born on the 27th January 1972 and is a Welsh singer and actor, known for his role as Go Compare man in the Gocompare.com insurance adverts on television. In 2010, Evans signed a six-album deal with Warner Music; his first album is called A Song in My Heart and was released on 21 March 2011. The album went straight to number one in the UK Classical Charts in the following week. In late 2011 Evans was cast as the opera singer Ubaldo Piangi, in the 25th Anniversary celebratory production of Andrew Lloyd Webber's The Phantom of the Opera at the Royal Albert Hall. Since 2009 Evans has starred in an advertising campaign for UK insurance comparison website Gocompare.com, playing the flamboyant, operatic tenor Gio Compario. In March 2015 Evans appeared in the Sky 1 comedy drama Stella, as a candidate running for council / Mexican wrestler. The episode ended with Evans singing a couple of numbers. In 2012 Evans presented The Guide to Opera on Classic FM.

Mark Anthony Patrick Owen was born on the 27th January 1972. Mark is an English singer and songwriter and was a member of pop-group Take That. After selecting Gary Barlow as the group's lead singer in 1989, Nigel Martin-Smith introduced Owen, Howard Donald, Jason Orange and finally Robbie Williams to the fold. The group were signed to RCA records, and after a number of top 40 hits, eventually secured their first number one with Barlow's "Pray". Previous hits included "A Million Love Songs", "It Only Takes a Minute" and "Could It Be Magic". The band's debut album Take That & Party was released on 17 August 1992. It reached number two on the UK Album Chart. After Take That split, Owen became the first of the band's ex-members to release a solo record. He reached number three in the UK Singles Chart with his debut single, "Child". His second single, "Clementine", also went to number three. In 1996 his album Green Man was released, charting at a number 33. After another single, "I Am What I Am", charted at number 29, Owen was dropped by BMG Records in late 1997.

Steven McManaman was born on the 11th February 1972 and is an English former footballer who played as a midfielder for Liverpool, Real Madrid and Manchester City. Steve McManaman was the most decorated English footballer to have played for a club abroad and is regarded as one of the best players of his generation, with the UEFA website stating in 2012 that "of all England's footballing exports in the modern era, none was as successful as McManaman". He is currently a co-commentator on ESPN and BT Sport's football coverage. After nine years at Liverpool, during which time he won the FA Cup and League Cup, McManaman moved to Real Madrid in 1999. The transfer became one of the most high-profile Bosman rulings of all time. He became the first English player to win the UEFA Champions League with a non-English club in 2000, and two years later became the first English player to win the Champions League twice. He retired from playing in 2005. Since his retirement, he has worked as a football pundit for Setanta Sports, ESPN and BT Sport.

Nicholas John Frost was born 28th March 1972 and is a British actor, comedian, screenwriter, producer, painter and author. He appeared in corporate training video clips such as "Chris Carter and the Coverplan Challenge", a Dixons sales video, before playing Tim's army-obsessed best friend Mike in Spaced (1999–2001), which aired on Channel 4 for two series. In 2004, he appeared in Shaun of the Dead, a "romantic zombie comedy", written by Simon Pegg and Spaced director Edgar Wright. Frost and Pegg appeared in a second Pegg-Wright feature film called Hot Fuzz, an action and cop genre homage, set in Gloucestershire. Frost plays bumbling Constable Danny Butterman, who partners up with Pegg's dynamic Nicholas Angel after the latter is transferred from the Metropolitan Police in London. The pair teamed up again for their self-penned 2011 science fiction comedy film Paul, whose storyline concerned a fugitive alien. In 2014, he played the eponymous character in the Sky Atlantic comedy, Mr. Sloane. In October 2015, Frost released a memoir titled Truths, Half Truths & Little White, detailing his life up to the age of 30.

James Edward Cracknell OBE was born 5th May 1972 is a British athlete, rowing champion and double Olympic gold medallist. James Cracknell began rowing whilst attending the independent Kingston Grammar School and rowed at the Junior World Championships in 1989 and 1990, winning a gold medal in 1990. In 1997, he won a seat in the men's coxless fours, with Steve Redgrave, Matthew Pinsent and Tim Foster. With this crew, he won the World Rowing Championships in 1997, 1998 and 1999 (with Ed Coode replacing the injured Foster), and finally the gold medal at the 2000 Summer Olympics. He ran the London Marathon on 23rd April 2006, in a time of 3 hours, finishing over an hour ahead of his rowing teammate Matthew Pinsent. In August 2009 Cracknell attempted to break the non-stop Land's End to John O'Groats mixed tandem world record along with Olympic gold medallist Rebecca Romero. The pair got just past Johnstone Bridge in Scotland before being forced to stop due to problems with Romero's knees. They were on course to break the record by over three hours.

Debra Stephenson was born 4th June 1972 and is an English actress, comedian, impressionist and singer. At the age of 14, Stephenson appeared on BBC TV's Opportunity Knocks, winning her way through to the All-Winners' Final, broadcast live from the London Palladium. Debra Stephenson was then on TV screens in 1998 in Kay Mellor's comedy drama about women's football, Playing the Field. In 1999, Stephenson had a more prominent role playing Shell Dockley in the ITV prison drama Bad Girls. Her performance as the psychotic Dockley earned her consecutive nominations for Best Actress at the National Television Awards in 1999 and 2000. After three years playing one of the show's most popular characters, Stephenson left in 2001, the same year she appeared in Lily Savage's Blankety Blank; she returned to Bad Girls for one last time in 2003. From June 2004 to December 2006, Stephenson starred in British soap opera Coronation Street playing Frankie Baldwin, the wife of Bradley Walsh's character, Danny. In September 2019 she made her debut as Jane in Midlife Cowboy, a new musical at the Pleasance Theatre written by Tony Hawks.

Jake Dylan Wood was born 12th July 1972 and is an English actor, known for his roles as Jackson and Max Branning in the BBC soap opera EastEnders. His first acting role was in the 1984 television series The Gentle Touch. In March 1990, Wood portrayed the role of Jackson in the BBC soap opera EastEnders, a minor character who met Diane Butcher (Sophie Lawrence) while she was sleeping rough on the streets of London. Wood was later cast to play the regular character Max Branning from June 2006 to present day. In 2014, Wood took part in the 12th series of Strictly Come Dancing. He was partnered with Janette Manrara, reaching the semi-final. In January 2018, Jake Wood started hosting a boxing podcast, Pound for Pound, with Spencer Oliver. In September 2020, it was announced that Jake would be departing from the cast of EastEnders after fifteen years in the role, with Max being written out as part of an "explosive exit". In January 2019, it was announced that he would be running the London Marathon with some of his EastEnders co-stars for a Dementia campaign in honour of Barbara Windsor.

Geraldine Estelle Horner (née Halliwell) was on the born 6th August 1972 and is an English singer, songwriter, author, actress, and philanthropist. She rose to prominence in the 1990s as Ginger Spice, a member of the pop girl group the Spice Girls. With over 85 million records sold worldwide, the group became the best-selling female group of all time. In 1999, Halliwell launched her solo career and released her debut studio album, Schizophonic, which spawned three number one singles including "Mi Chico Latino", "Lift Me Up", and "Bag It Up", while the lead single, "Look at Me", peaked at number two. After a few years of relative obscurity, in April 2010, Halliwell announced that she had started working on new music. Halliwell began dating Christian Horner, the team principal of the Red Bull Racing Formula One team in February 2014. They announced their engagement on 11th November 2014, and the couple were married on 15th May 2015 at St Mary's Church in Woburn, Bedfordshire.

Idrissa Akuna Elba OBE was born on the 6th September 1972 and is an English actor, writer, producer, rapper, singer, songwriter and DJ. He is known for roles including Stringer Bell in the HBO series The Wire, DCI John Luther in the BBC One series Luther, and Nelson Mandela in the biographical film Mandela: Long Walk to Freedom (2013). He has been nominated four times for a Golden Globe Award for Best Actor – Miniseries or Television Film, winning one, and was nominated five times for a Primetime Emmy Award. In October 2014, Elba presented the series Journey Dot Africa with Idris Elba on BBC Radio 2, exploring all types of African music. Elba has also featured in various television commercials for Sky box-sets in 2013, 2014, 2015, 2016, and 2019. In January 2016, Elba addressed the UK Parliament in regards to the concern of the lack of diversity on screen. Stating, 'Change is coming but it's taking its sweet time', he spoke about the lack of diversity regarding race, gender and sexuality. Elba hosted The Best FIFA Football Awards 2017 at the London Palladium on 23 October 2017. During the show he took a selfie of "the best team in the world" which included Lionel Messi, Cristiano Ronaldo and Neymar.

Natasha Margaret Kaplinsky OBE was born on the 9th September 1972 and is an English newsreader, TV presenter and journalist, best known for her roles as a studio anchor on Sky News, BBC News, Channel 5 and ITV News. After two years at Sky News, Kaplinsky joined BBC News in 2001 where she co-hosted Breakfast until 2005, when she became the host of the Six O'clock News. In October 2007, Kaplinsky was recruited to help relaunch Five reportedly for the highest fee ever paid to a UK newsreader, where she presented a new look, retitled Five News with Natasha Kaplinsky for three years. After leaving Channel 5, she went on to join ITV News as a presenter. She was also the subject of the most highly rated Who Do You Think You Are. She is perhaps most famous for being the first ever winner of the first series of BBC's Strictly Come Dancing in 2004. In 2014 the then PM David Cameron asked Kaplinsky to become a Holocaust Commissioner leading a project to interview 112 survivors. She was awarded an OBE in 2017 for her services to the Holocaust Commission. Natasha Kaplinsky has co-founded a mother and baby company, Mum & You.

William John Paul Gallagher was born on 21st September 1972 and is an English singer and songwriter. He was the lead singer of the rock band Oasis from 1991 to 2009 and the rock band Beady Eye from 2009 to 2014 before releasing his debut solo album in 2017. Gallagher's debut solo album, As You Were, was released in October 2017 and proved to be a critical and commercial success. It topped the UK Albums Chart and was the ninth fastest-selling debut album of the 2010s in the UK, with over 103,000 units sold in its first week. In 2018, the album was certified Platinum with over 300,000 units sold in the UK. One of the most recognisable figures in British music, Gallagher is noted for his outspoken and abrasive manner, penchant for wearing parkas, and distinctive singing style. His attitude during Oasis' commercially peak years in the 1990s garnered attention from the British tabloid press, which often ran stories concerning his alleged drug use and behaviour. In March 2010, Gallagher was voted the greatest frontman of all time in a reader poll by Q magazine. In 2019, he received the MTV Europe Music Award for "Rock Icon" award.

Samantha Zoe Womack was born on the 2nd November 1972 and is a British actress, singer, model and director who have worked in film, television and stage. The actress first came to prominence in March 1991 aged 18, when she won the annual A Song for Europe competition to represent the United Kingdom in the Eurovision Song Contest. She finished joint tenth and the song, "A Message to Your Heart", peaked at number 30 on the UK Singles Chart. From 1994 to 1998 Womack played Mandy in the BBC Two sitcom Game On opposite Ben Chaplin. She remained on the show until its end in 1998. On the 11th May 2007 it was announced that she would be joining EastEnders as Ronnie Mitchell, a cousin of the well-known Mitchell brothers. She had previously appeared in the soap in a minor role as a girlfriend of Simon Wicks. Womack made her final appearance as Ronnie on 7th July 2011 when the character was sent to prison. In May 2013, it was confirmed that Womack would return to EastEnders as Ronnie Mitchell. Womack's character Ronnie Mitchell was later killed off on the episode broadcast 1st January 2017 when she was trying to save Roxy Mitchell from drowning and drowned herself.

SPORTING EVENTS 1972

1972 County Cricket Season

The 1972 County Championship was the 73rd officially organised running of the County Championship, and ran from the 3rd May to the 12th September 1972. Warwickshire County Cricket Club claimed their third title. There was an increase in limited overs cricket with the introduction of the Benson & Hedges Cup, which was part mini-league and part knockout along the lines of soccer's World Cup competition. It caused another reduction in the number of County Championship matches and the B&H (as it was often called) was never popular among cricket's traditional followers. The tournament lasted until 2002, after which it was effectively replaced by Twenty20. The County Championship was won by Warwickshire for the third time in their history.

Team	Pld	W	L	D	D1	A	BatBP	BowBP	Pts
Warwickshire (C)	20	9	0	11	0	0	68	69	227
Kent	20	7	4	9	0	0	69	52	191
Gloucestershire	20	7	4	9	0	0	38	77	185
Northamptonshire	20	7	3	10	0	0	34	77	181
Essex	20	6	4	10	0	0	50	63	173
Leicestershire	20	6	2	12	0	0	43	68	171
Worcestershire	20	4	4	12	0	0	59	68	167
Middlesex	20	5	5	10	0	0	48	61	159
Hampshire	20	4	6	10	0	0	50	64	154
Yorkshire	20	4	5	10	1	0	39	73	152
Somerset	20	4	2	14	0	0	34	71	145
Surrey	20	3	5	12	0	0	49	61	140
Glamorgan	20	1	7	12	0	0	55	61	126
Nottinghamshire	20	1	6	13	0	0	38	73	121
Lancashire	20	2	3	14	0	1	41	57	118
Sussex	20	2	8	10	0	0	46	49	115
Derbyshire	20	1	5	12	1	1	27	60	97

1971–72 in English football

Brian Clough, 37, won the first major trophy of his managerial career by guiding Derby County to their first league championship. They overcame Leeds United, Liverpool and Manchester City to win a four-horse race, with only a single point separating them. It was so close that when Manchester City won their last game of the season – against Derby on 22nd April 1972 – they were top of the league by a point but had no chance of being champions, as Derby and Liverpool both had games in hand, were still to play each other, and both boasted a superior goal average to City's. Although Derby beat Liverpool to pass Manchester City at the top of the table, Liverpool (two points back) and Leeds (one point back) each still had a game left.

Leeds, who had won the FA Cup for the first time of their history, could have completed the double by avoiding defeat against Wolverhampton Wanderers, but instead lost 2–1. Liverpool could also have overtaken Derby by defeating Arsenal, but could muster only a 0–0 draw. This assured Derby the title by a single point.

Pos	Team	Pld	W	D	L	GF	GA	GR	Pts	Qualification or relegation
1	Derby County	42	24	10	8	69	33	2.091	58	Qualified for the European Cup
2	Leeds United	42	24	9	9	73	31	2.355	57	Qualified for the Cup Winners' Cup
3	Liverpool	42	24	9	9	64	30	2.133	57	Qualified for the UEFA Cup
4	Manchester City	42	23	11	8	77	45	1.711	57	
5	Arsenal	42	22	8	12	58	40	1.450	52	
6	Tottenham Hotspur	42	19	13	10	63	42	1.500	51	Qualified for the UEFA Cup
7	Chelsea	42	18	12	12	58	49	1.184	48	
8	Manchester United	42	19	10	13	69	61	1.131	48	
9	Wolverhampton Wanderers	42	18	11	13	65	57	1.140	47	
10	Sheffield United	42	17	12	13	61	60	1.017	46	
11	Newcastle United	42	15	11	16	49	52	0.942	41	
12	Leicester City	42	13	13	16	41	46	0.891	39	
13	Ipswich Town	42	11	16	15	39	53	0.736	38	
14	West Ham United	42	12	12	18	47	51	0.922	36	
15	Everton	42	9	18	15	37	48	0.771	36	
16	West Bromwich Albion	42	12	11	19	42	54	0.778	35	
17	Stoke City	42	10	15	17	39	56	0.696	35	Qualified for the UEFA Cup
18	Coventry City	42	9	15	18	44	67	0.657	33	
19	Southampton	42	12	7	23	52	80	0.650	31	
20	Crystal Palace	42	8	13	21	39	65	0.600	29	
21	Nottingham Forest	42	8	9	25	47	81	0.580	25	Relegated to the Second Division
22	Huddersfield Town	42	6	13	23	27	59	0.458	25	

1971–72 Scottish Division One

The 1971–72 Scottish Division One was won by Celtic by ten points over nearest rival Aberdeen. Clyde and Dunfermline finished 17th and 18th respectively and were relegated to the 1972–73 Second Division.

Celtic is one of only five clubs in the world to have won over 100 trophies in their history. The club has won the Scottish league championship 51 times, most recently in 2019–20, the Scottish Cup 40 times and the Scottish League Cup 19 times. The club's greatest season was 1966–67, when Celtic became the first British team to win the European Cup, also winning the Scottish league championship, the Scottish Cup, the League Cup and the Glasgow Cup. Celtic also reached the 1970 European Cup Final and the 2003 UEFA Cup Final, losing in both.

Division 1

Pos	Team	Pld	W	D	L	GF	GA	GD	Pts	Qualification or relegation
1	Celtic	34	28	4	2	96	28	+68	60	Champion
2	Aberdeen	34	21	8	5	80	26	+54	50	
3	Rangers	34	21	2	11	71	38	+33	44	
4	Hibernian	34	19	6	9	62	34	+28	44	
5	Dundee	34	14	13	7	59	38	+21	41	
6	Heart of Midlothian	34	13	13	8	53	49	+4	39	
7	Partick Thistle	34	12	10	12	53	54	−1	34	
8	St Johnstone	34	12	8	14	52	58	−6	32	
9	Dundee United	34	12	7	15	55	70	−15	31	
10	Motherwell	34	11	7	16	49	69	−20	29	
11	Kilmarnock	34	11	6	17	49	64	−15	28	
12	Ayr United	34	9	10	15	40	58	−18	28	
13	Morton	34	10	7	17	46	52	−6	27	
14	Falkirk	34	10	7	17	44	60	−16	27	
15	Airdrieonians	34	7	12	15	44	76	−32	26	
16	East Fife	34	5	15	14	34	61	−27	25	
17	Clyde	34	7	10	17	33	66	−33	24	Relegated to 1972–73 Second Division
18	Dunfermline Athletic	34	7	9	18	31	50	−19	23	

1972 Five Nations Championship

The 1972 Five Nations Championship was the forty-third series of the rugby union Five Nations Championship. Including the previous incarnations as the Home Nations and Five Nations, this was the seventy-eighth series of the northern hemisphere rugby union championship. The championship was not completed for the first time since World War II.

Scotland and Wales did not travel to Dublin to play Ireland because of the escalating political situation. Although the remaining fixtures of the schedule were fulfilled, as both Ireland and Wales won all their matches, neither could claim the title. To fill the gap of the missing two fixtures, France played a friendly match in Dublin (in addition to the scheduled match in Paris).

In total nine matches were played between 15th January and 29th April. It was contested by England, France, Ireland, Scotland and Wales.

This was the first Five Nations Championship where a try was worth four points.

Scotland wins the Calcutta Cup beating England 29 – 3.

Teams

Nation	Venue	City	Head coach	Captain
England	Twickenham	London	John Elders	Bob Hiller/Peter Dixon
France	Stade Olympique Yves-du-Manoir	Colombes	Fernand Cazenave	Benoit Dauga/Walter Spanghero/Pierre Villepreux
Ireland	Lansdowne Road	Dublin	Syd Millar	Tom Kiernan
Scotland	Murrayfield	Edinburgh	Bill Dickinson	Peter Brown
Wales	Cardiff Arms Park	Cardiff	Clive Rowlands	John Lloyd

Table

Position	Nation	Games				Points			Table points
		Played	Won	Drawn	Lost	For	Against	Difference	
1	Wales	3	3	0	0	67	21	+46	6
2	Ireland	2	2	0	0	30	21	+9	4
3	Scotland	3	2	0	1	55	53	+2	4
4	France	4	1	0	3	61	66	−5	2
5	England	4	0	0	4	36	88	−52	0

Top point scorer(s)	Barry John (32)
Top try scorer(s)	Bernard Duprat (4)

The Masters 1972

The 1972 Masters Tournament was the 36th Masters Tournament, held April 6–9 at Augusta National Golf Club in Augusta, Georgia.

Jack Nicklaus opened with a 68 and led wire-to-wire to win the fourth of his six Masters titles, three strokes ahead of three runners-up. It was the tenth of 18 major titles as a professional for Nicklaus, who also won the U.S. Open in 1972 and was the runner-up at the Open Championship in Scotland, one stroke behind Lee Trevino.

It was the first Masters played without founder Bobby Jones, who died in December 1971 at age 69. The 1972 Masters was also the debut of 20 year old University of Texas golfer and future two-time champion Ben Crenshaw who was low amateur at 295 (T19).

Banned from the last five Masters, commentator Jack Whitaker returned to the CBS telecast in 1972. At the end of the 18-hole Monday playoff in 1966, he had referred to the portion of the gallery trailing the players as a "mob."

Nicklaus became the third wire-to-wire winner in Masters history following Craig Wood in 1941 and Arnold Palmer in 1960. Through 2016, there have been five; the next were Raymond Floyd in 1976 and Jordan Spieth in 2015.

Place	Player	Country	Score	To par	Money ($)
1	**Jack Nicklaus**	United States	68-71-73-74=286	-2	25,000
T2	Bruce Crampton	Australia	72-75-69-73=289	+1	15,833
	Bobby Mitchell	United States	73-72-71-73=289		
	Tom Weiskopf	United States	74-71-70-74=289		
T5	Homero Blancas	United States	76-71-69-74=290	+2	6,200
	Bruce Devlin	Australia	74-75-70-71=290		
	Jerry Heard	United States	73-71-72-74=290		
	Jim Jamieson	United States	72-70-71-77=290		
	Jerry McGee	United States	73-74-71-72=290		
10	Gary Player	South Africa	73-75-72-71=291	+3	3,600
	Dave Stockton	United States	76-70-74-71=291		

Between 1971 and 1980, Jack Nicklaus won nine more major championships, overtook Bobby Jones's record of 13 majors, and became the first player to complete double and triple career grand slams. He won the 1986 Masters, his 18th and final major championship at age 46, the tournament's oldest winner.

Grand National 1972

The 1972 Grand National was the 126th renewal of the Grand National horse race that took place at Aintree near Liverpool, England, on 8 April 1972. The winner was Well To Do, whose price went down from 33–1 to 14-1 the day before. Former winner Gay Trip was second, and there was a dead-heat for third place. The winning colours of Capt. Tim Forster were - crimson, gold sleeves, hooped cap.

Position	Name	Jockey	Age	Handicap (st-lb)	SP
01	Well To Do	Graham Thorner	9	10-1	14/1
02	Gay Trip	Terry Biddlecombe	10	11-9	12/1
03	Black Secret	Sean Barker	8	11-2	14/1

2,000 Guineas 1972

High Top was a British Thoroughbred racehorse and sire, best known for winning the classic 2000 Guineas in 1972. High Top was one of the leading British two-year-olds of 1971 when his successes included a defeat of a strong field tin the Observer Gold Cup. After winning a trial race on his first appearance of 1972 he led from the start to beat the future Epsom Derby winner Roberto in the 2000 Guineas. His classic win was the first of seventeen British classic winners ridden by Willie Carson. High Top never won again but finished a close second in both the Sussex Stakes and the Prix Jacques Le Marois. At the end of the year he was retired to stud and became an extremely successful breeding stallion.

St Leger 1972

Boucher wins St Leger. Boucher was an American-bred, Irish-trained Thoroughbred racehorse and sire. In Ireland he won the Beresford Stakes as a two-year-old in 1971 and went on to win the Nijinsky Stakes and the Desmond Stakes in 1972. In September 1972 he was sent to England where he won the St. Leger Stakes at Doncaster. In the St Leger at Doncaster, Boucher started at odds of 3/1 against six opponents, with the Irish Derby winner, Steel Pulse, being made the 9/4 favourite. Ridden by Lester Piggott he moved up to challenge for the lead two furlongs from the finish and won after a struggle by half a length from Our Mirage, with The Oaks winner Ginevra four lengths further back in third. The race was run on extremely soft ground and the winning time of 3:28.71 was the slowest recorded at Doncaster in the 20th century. At the end of the season he was retired to stand as a stallion in Australia, where he had some success as a sire of winners.

The Derby 1972

Roberto wins the Epsom Derby. Roberto was an American-bred, Irish-trained Thoroughbred Champion racehorse. In a career that lasted from 1971 until July 1973 he ran fourteen times and won seven races. He was the best Irish two-year-old of 1971, when his victories included the National Stakes. As a three-year-old, he won the Derby before recording his most famous victory when beating Brigadier Gerard in the inaugural running of the Benson and Hedges Gold Cup. This is regarded by many experts to have been one of the greatest ever performances on a European racecourse. He won the Coronation Cup as a four-year-old before being retired to stud. Roberto required a left-handed track to perform to his best; he never won going right-handed. He was described by Lester Piggott as "a champion when things were in his favour". Roberto also proved to be a highly successful and influential stallion.

British Grand Prix 1972

The 1972 British Grand Prix (formally the John Player Grand Prix) was a Formula One motor race held at Brands Hatch on 15th July 1972. It was race 7 of 12 in both the 1972 World Championship of Drivers and the 1972 International Cup for Formula One Manufacturers. The race was won by Brazilian driver Emerson Fittipaldi driving a Lotus 72D.
Ronnie Peterson suffered an engine failure with less than two laps to go, and crashed into the parked cars of Graham Hill and François Cevert.

Jacky Ickx took pole position with a time of 1m.22.2secs.

Brands Hatch Circuit is a motor racing circuit in West Kingsdown, Kent, England, United Kingdom. Originally used as a grass track motorcycle circuit on farmland, it hosted 12 runnings of the British Grand Prix between 1964 and 1986 and currently hosts many British and International racing events. The venue is owned and operated by Jonathan Palmer's MotorSport Vision organisation.

Final Placings

Pos	No	Driver	Constructor	Laps	Time/Retired	Grid	Points
1	8	🇧🇷 Emerson Fittipaldi	Lotus-Ford	76	1:47:50.2	2	9
2	1	🇬🇧 Jackie Stewart	Tyrrell-Ford	76	+ 4.1	4	6
3	19	🇺🇸 Peter Revson	McLaren-Ford	76	+ 1:12.5	3	4
4	17	Chris Amon	Matra	75	+ 1 Lap	17	3
5	18	Denny Hulme	McLaren-Ford	75	+ 1 Lap	11	2
6	6	Arturo Merzario	Ferrari	75	+ 1 Lap	9	1

1972 Wimbledon Championships

The 1972 Wimbledon Championships was a tennis tournament that took place on the outdoor grass courts at the All England Lawn Tennis and Croquet Club in Wimbledon, London, United Kingdom. The tournament was scheduled to be held from Monday 26th June until Saturday 8th July 1972 but rain on the final Saturday meant that the men's singles, women's doubles and mixed doubles finals were played on Sunday 9th July. It was the first time in the tournament's history that finals were played on a Sunday. It was the 86th staging of the Wimbledon Championships, and the third Grand Slam tennis event of 1972.

Men's Singles

Stan Smith defeated Ilie Năstase in the final, 4–6, 6–3, 6–3, 4–6, 7–5 to win the Gentlemen's Singles tennis title at the 1972 Wimbledon Championships. It was Smith's only Wimbledon singles title, and his second, and final, Grand Slam singles title.

Women's Singles

Billie Jean King defeated the defending champion Evonne Goolagong in the final, 6–3, 6–3 to win the Ladies' Singles tennis title at the 1972 Wimbledon Championships.

Men's Doubles

Roy Emerson and Rod Laver were prevented from defending their title due to the International Lawn Tennis Federation ban on World Championship Tennis contract players competing in their tournaments. Bob Hewitt and Frew McMillan defeated Arthur Ashe and Dennis Ralston in the final, 4–6, 9–7, 6–8, 6–4, 6–4 to win the Gentlemen's Doubles title at the 1972 Wimbledon Championships.

Women's Doubles

Rosie Casals and Billie Jean King were the defending champions, but decided not to play together. Casals partnered with Virginia Wade but lost in the semi-finals to Judy Dalton and Françoise Dürr. King and her partner Betty Stöve defeated Dalton and Dürr in the final, 6–2, 4–6, 6–3 to win the Ladies' Doubles tennis title at the 1972 Wimbledon Championships.

Mixed Doubles

Owen Davidson and Billie Jean King were the defending champions, but Davidson did not compete. King partnered with Clark Graebner but lost in the semi-finals to Ilie Năstase and Rosie Casals. Năstase and Casals defeated Kim Warwick and Evonne Goolagong in the final, 6–4, 6–4 to win the Mixed Doubles tennis title at the 1972 Wimbledon Championships.

Stan Smith

Billie Jean King

Watership Down is a survival and adventure novel by English author Richard Adams, published by Rex Collings Ltd of London in 1972. Set in southern England, around Hampshire, the story features a small group of rabbits. Although they live in their natural wild environment, with burrows, they are anthropomorphised, possessing their own culture, language, proverbs, poetry, and mythology. Evoking epic themes, the novel follows the rabbits as they escape the destruction of their warren and seek a place to establish a new home (the hill of Watership Down), encountering perils and temptations along the way. Watership Down was Richard Adams' debut novel. It was rejected by several publishers before Collings accepted the manuscript; the published book then won the annual Carnegie Medal (UK), annual Guardian Prize (UK), and other book awards. The novel was adapted into an animated feature film in 1978 and, from 1999 to 2001, an animated children's television series. In 2018, a miniseries of the story was made, which both aired in the UK and was made available on Netflix.

Adams completed a sequel almost 25 years later, in 1996, Tales from Watership Down, constructed as a collection of 19 short stories about El-ahrairah and the rabbits of the Watership Down warren.

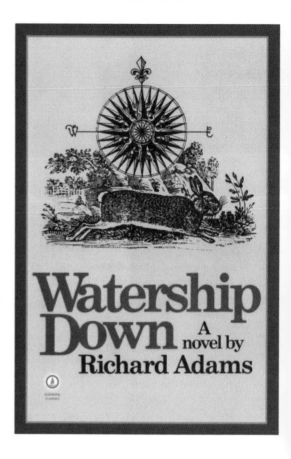

Elephants Can Remember is a work of detective fiction by British writer Agatha Christie, first published in 1972. It features her Belgian detective Hercule Poirot and the recurring character Ariadne Oliver. This was the last novel to feature either character, although it was succeeded by Curtain: Poirot's Last Case, which had been written in the early 1940s but was published last. Elephants Can Remember concentrates on memory and oral testimony.

At a literary luncheon Ariadne Oliver is approached by a woman named Mrs Burton-Cox, whose son Desmond is engaged to Oliver's goddaughter Celia Ravenscroft. Mrs Burton-Cox questions the truth regarding the deaths of Celia's parents. Fourteen years before, Oliver's close school friend Margaret Ravenscroft and her husband, General Alistair Ravenscroft, were found dead near their manor house in Overcliffe. Both had been shot with a revolver found between their bodies, which bore only their fingerprints.

The investigation into their deaths found it impossible to determine if it was a double suicide, or if one of them murdered the other and then committed suicide. Their deaths left Celia and another child orphaned. After consulting Celia, Mrs Oliver invites her friend Hercule Poirot to resolve the issue.

Pure, White and Deadly is a 1972 book by John Yudkin, a British nutritionist and former Chair of Nutrition at Queen Elizabeth College, London. Published in New York, it was the first publication by a scientist to anticipate the adverse health effects, especially in relation to obesity and heart disease, of the public's increased sugar consumption. At the time of publication, Yudkin sat on the advisory panel of the British Department of Health's Committee on the Medical Aspects of Food and Nutrition Policy (COMA). He stated his intention in writing the book in the last paragraph of the first chapter: "I hope that when you have read this book I shall have convinced you that sugar is really dangerous."

The book and author suffered a barrage of criticism at the time, particularly from the sugar industry, processed-food manufacturers, and Ancel Keys, an American physiologist who argued in favour of restricting dietary fat, not sugar, and who sought to ridicule Yudkin's work. Two further editions of the book were published, the second after Yudkin's death in 1995. An expanded version appeared in 1986, revised by Yudkin himself, to include much additional research evidence. In 2012 the book was re-published by Penguin Books with a new introduction by Robert Lustig to reflect the changed nutritional context that the book had helped to create.

The Problem of Sugar

Charlie and the Great Glass Elevator is a children's book by British author Roald Dahl. It is the sequel to Charlie and the Chocolate Factory, continuing the story of young Charlie Bucket and chocolatier Willy Wonka as they travel in the Great Glass Elevator. The book was first published in the United States by Alfred A. Knopf, Inc. in 1972 and in the United Kingdom by George Allen & Unwin in 1973.

The story picks up where the previous book left off, with Charlie and family aboard the flying Great Glass Elevator. The Elevator accidentally goes into orbit, and Mr. Wonka docks them at the Space Hotel USA. Their interception of the hotel is mistaken by approaching astronauts and hotel staff in a Commuter Capsule and listeners on Earth (including the President of the United States) as an act of space piracy and they are variously accused of being enemy agents, spies and aliens. Shortly after their arrival, they discover that the hotel has been overrun by dangerous, shape-changing alien monsters known as The Vermicious Knids. The Knids cannot resist showing off and reveal themselves by using the five hotel elevators (with one Knid in each of them) and spell out the word "SCRAM", giving the group time to evacuate. As the group leaves, a Knid follows the Great Glass Elevator and tries to break it open, but to no avail, which results in the Knid receiving a bruise on its backside and hungering for payback.

The Fire People is a historical novel by Alexander Cordell, first published in 1972. It forms part of the 'Second Welsh Trilogy' of Cordell's writings. It tells of events leading up to the 1831 Merthyr Rising in Merthyr Tydfil and surrounding areas in South Wales.

In 1830. Merthyr Tydfil is the largest town in Wales; an industrial centre and one of the Top Towns, with four major iron works. People from all parts of the world flock to find work there; from Spain and Italy, from England, and from Ireland. Men and Women work alongside each other, doing equally heavy and dangerous jobs, frequently dying at the workplace.

Gideon Davies is a former worker at Taibach copper works and a trained musician. After losing nearly all his sight in an accident at the works, he is now an itinerant musician, playing his fiddle at taverns, wakes and social gatherings throughout South Wales. He also uses his travels to promote the concept of unions and worker's rights. Various other characters are also travelling to Merthyr, attracted by the coal and iron industries. They include the genteel Miss Thrush the Sweets who has sold her shop in Pontypridd, and is secretly enamoured of Gideon, even though she only sees him about once a year.

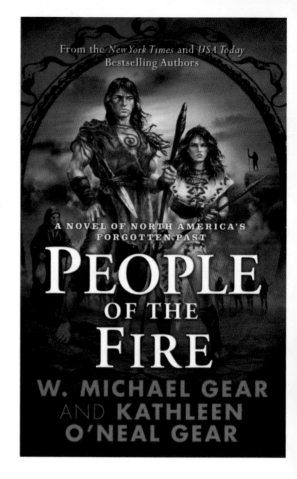

From the *New York Times* and *USA Today* Bestselling Authors

A NOVEL OF NORTH AMERICA'S FORGOTTEN PAST

PEOPLE OF THE FIRE

W. MICHAEL GEAR AND KATHLEEN O'NEAL GEAR

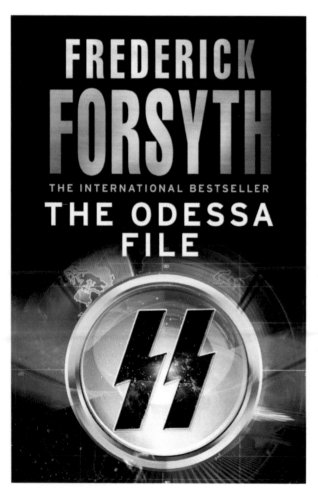

FREDERICK FORSYTH

THE INTERNATIONAL BESTSELLER

THE ODESSA FILE

The Odessa File is a thriller by Frederick Forsyth, first published in 1972, about the adventures of a young German reporter attempting to discover the location of a former SS concentration-camp commander. The name ODESSA is an acronym for the German phrase "Organisation der ehemaligen SS-Angehörigen", which translates as "Organisation of Former Members of the SS". The novel alleges that ODESSA was an international Nazi organisation established before the defeat of Nazi Germany for the purpose of protecting former members of the SS after the war.

In November 1963, shortly after the assassination of John F. Kennedy, Peter Miller, a German freelance crime reporter, follows an ambulance to the apartment of Salomon Tauber, a Holocaust survivor who has committed suicide. The next day, Miller is given the dead man's diary by a friend in the Bundespolizei. After reading Tauber's life story and learning that Tauber had been in the Riga Ghetto commanded by Eduard Roschmann, "The Butcher of Riga", Miller resolves to search for Roschmann whom Tauber recognised a few days earlier, alive and prosperous, in Hamburg. Miller's attention is especially drawn to one diary passage in which Tauber describes having seen Roschmann shoot a German Army captain who was wearing a distinctive military decoration.

Pearls, Girls and Monty Bodkin is a comic novel by P. G. Wodehouse, first published in the United Kingdom on 12 October 1972 by Barrie & Jenkins, and in the United States on 6 August 1973 by Simon & Schuster, Inc. under the title The Plot That Thickened. Although written towards the end of the Wodehouse's life, and published 37 years after the The Luck of the Bodkins (1935), the events of book follow on directly from those recounted in the earlier novel. Monty Bodkin's fiancée Gertrude Butterwick refuses to marry without the consent of her father J. B. Butterwick. He dislikes Monty and will not agree to the match unless Monty can remain gainfully employed for a full year. Having spent a year working as a production advisor for the Superba-Llewellyn Motion Picture Corporation in Hollywood, Monty now returns to England. However, Butterwick insists that the job did not count because Monty got it (in The Luck of the Bodkins) through dishonest means.

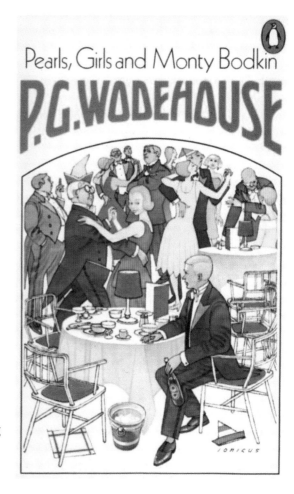

To appease Butterwick, Monty seeks another paid position. Sally Miller (secretly in love with Monty) falsely tells her employer Grayce Llewellyn that Monty comes from an aristocratic family, and Grayce appoints Monty as secretary to her husband, Ivor Llewellyn, who is now in England. Monty is to work at the Llewellyns' newly-rented country house, Mellingham Hall in Sussex, where Llewellyn is writing a history of his film studio.

Rule Britannia is Daphne du Maurier's last novel, published in 1972 by Victor Gollancz. The novel is set in a fictional near future in which the UK's recent withdrawal from the EEC has brought the country to the verge of bankruptcy.

Emma, 20, lives with her elderly grandmother, Mad (short for 'Madam'), a famous retired actress, in the small village of Poldrea in Cornwall. They share a large house near the coast with Mad's six 'maladjusted' adopted sons who range in age from 3 to 18. One morning, Emma wakes to the sound of aeroplanes overhead. An American warship has anchored in the bay and United States Marines are marching over the fields. They are trigger-happy, and one of them shoots and kills a local farmer's dog.

After some hours of civil confusion, a TV announcement is made by the prime minister: due to recent economic and military failures on the continent, the UK and the USA have joined together as a single nation, to be called USUK. The new government of USUK declares a state of emergency, institute's roadblocks, and cuts local telephone and postal communication. To Mad and her family the US Marines appear less like invited friends than a hostile invading force.

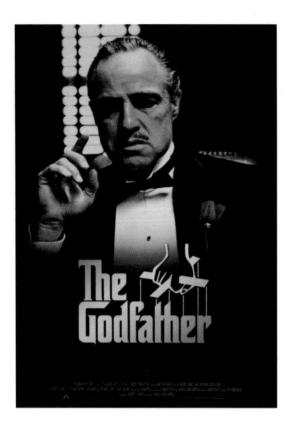

The Godfather "Don" Vito Corleone is the head of the Corleone mafia family in New York. He is at the event of his daughter's wedding. Michael, Vito's youngest son and a decorated WW II Marine is also present at the wedding. Michael seems to be uninterested in being a part of the family business. Vito is a powerful man, and is kind to all those who give him respect but is ruthless against those who do not. But when a powerful and treacherous rival wants to sell drugs and needs the Don's influence for the same, Vito refuses to do it. What follows is a clash between Vito's fading old values and the new ways which may cause Michael to do the thing he was most reluctant in doing and wage a mob war against all the other mafia families which could tear the Corleone family apart.

Winner of three Oscars for

Best Picture:	**Al Ruddy**
Best Writing:	**Mario Puzo**
	Francis Ford Coppola
Best Actor:	**Marlon Brando**

Run time is 2h 55mins

Trivia

During an early shot of the scene where Vito Corleone returns home and his people carry him up the stairs, Marlon Brando put weights under his body on the bed as a prank, to make it harder to lift him.

James Caan improvised the part where he throws the FBI photographer's camera to the ground. The actor's frightened reaction is genuine. Caan also came up with the idea of throwing money at the man to make up for breaking his camera. As he put it, "Where I came from, you broke something, you replaced it or repaid the owner."

The scene where Sonny beats up Carlo (Connie's husband) took four days to shoot, and featured more than 700 extras. The use of the garbage can lid was improvised by James Caan.

Goofs

When Michael finds his father without protection in the hospital, he picks up the phone by the bed to alert the family. The receiver has a curly cord which wasn't available until the mid- to late-1950s.

At the airport at night, a swept tail Cessna 182 is shown. Production of this airplane didn't start until approximately the mid-1960s.

In several scenes, wine bottles are shown with the DOC Italian wine classification designation shown on the bottle. DOC designations did not come in effect until 1963.

In late 1945, the Empire State Building is shown with the 222-foot television antenna mast that it did not acquire until 1950.

"What's Up Doc?" This is the comic tale of four identical pieces of red plaid luggage and one San Francisco hotel, in the spirit of Howard Hawks but made by Peter Bogdanovich. One bag contains secret government files, another has expensive jewels and a third has igneous rocks. It is unclear what is in the fourth bag, carried by the would-be erudite Judy Maxwell...but all four bags end up at the Hotel Bristol. Judy has a yen for food and Dr. Howard Bannister and no "off" button. Dr. Bannister (deliciously deadpan and hunky, Ryan O'Neal) has a yen for igneous rock formations. When all four bags are hopelessly mixed up and Eunice, Howard's prim and bossy fiancé (unforgettably played by Madeline Kahn) is kidnapped, only the long arm of the law, (i.e. the judiciary), can make any sense of the chaos. There are no palaeontologists or tigers but there are madcap antics, the obligatory San Francisco chase scenes and several clever one-liners.

Box Office
Budget:$4,000,000 (estimated)
Gross USA: $66,000,000

Run time 1h 34mins

Trivia
First American film to credit the stunt people in the credits (first British film to do so was the James Bond film Moonraker (1979)).

The long-haired blond delivery boy whose bike Judy steals is played by Kevin O'Neal, Ryan O'Neal's brother. The woman she sits next to on the plane in the final scene is Patricia O'Neal, their mother.

The pizza restaurant where Judy Maxwell watches pizzas being made was a real pizza restaurant at the time and remains virtually the same to this day. It's located at Bush St. on the corner of Jones.

The movie premiered at the 6,000 seat Radio City Music Hall Theatre in New York City in 1972. The film's first 2 weekends broke the house record that had stood since 1933.

Goofs
While Eunice decides to take Howard's rocks back to his room, she hurriedly puts her wig on and it teeters on her head messily. When she opens her door and walks down the hall, her wig is neat and fitting perfectly.

When Mr. Jones is following Mr. Smith at the beginning of the movie. Mr. Jones gets into a cab where the cab driver is very noticeably bald. But when he gets out later on, the cab driver has a lot of hair blowing in the breeze.

Throughout the film Howard strikes several rocks with tuning forks, and then listens to the tuning fork as if he's expecting a different tone when he hits different rocks. Tuning forks are made to resonate at a fixed pitch, so no matter what object is struck with the fork, it will always sound the same.

Hotel Manager escorts Howard to call an elevator, whereupon fingers are clearly visible sliding said elevator door open, and are visible again upon closing.

Last Tango In Paris. Crazed with grief after his wife commits suicide, Paul, an American expatriate, roams the streets of Paris until, while apartment hunting, he faces Jeanne, an unknown girl across an empty room. Brutally, without a word, he rapes the soon-compliant stranger. It should have been hit-and-run sex, but Paul stays at the scene of the erotic accident. While arranging his wife's funeral, Paul leases the apartment where he is to meet the puzzled girl for a series of frenzied afternoons. "No names here," he roughly tells her, setting up the rules of the game. They are to shut out the world outside, forfeit their pasts and their identities. Paul degrades Jeanne in every possible way, levelling all her inhibitions into sheer brutality. Paul is soon dissatisfied with mere possession of her body; he must also have her mind. When she rejects his mad love to enter a comfortable marriage with her dull fiancé, Paul finally confesses: "I love you, you dummy."

Box Office
Budget:$1,250,000 (estimated)
Gross USA: $36,144,000
Cumulative Worldwide Gross: $36,182,181

Run time 2h 09mins.

Trivia

After the film's release in Europe, director Bernardo Bertolucci, producer Alberto Grimaldi, Marlon Brando and Maria Schneider were all indicted by a court in Bologna, Italy for making the film under the term "utilitarian pornography." They were all acquitted of the charge shortly thereafter, with Bertolucci losing his civil rights (including his right to vote) for five years.

This film was banned in Chile for nearly thirty years. It was also banned in its country of origin, Italy, until 1987.

Maria Schneider gave frank interviews in wake of the film's controversy. She claimed that she had slept with fifty men and seventy women, that she was "bisexual completely," and that she used heroin, cocaine and marijuana.

As the film was banned in Spain, the town of Perpignan on the French-Spanish border was besieged with visitors crossing the border to see it.

Goofs

The bottle of "bourbon" is actually Jack Daniels' Tennessee whiskey. Since the Daniels distillery is not in the Bourbon region of Kentucky that whiskey cannot be called "bourbon" according to US law.

In the final scene, as the camera pulls away from the balcony, you can clearly see a crew member and a lighting array reflected in the glass panel of the right balcony door.

When Jeanne disappears during her bridal gown fitting, Tom goes running down the street to find her in the pouring rain. As he gets about fifty feet from the camera he sudden runs into a section of the street that is dry and there is no rain coming down. He apparently ran past the maximum range of the rain making equipment they were using for the shot.

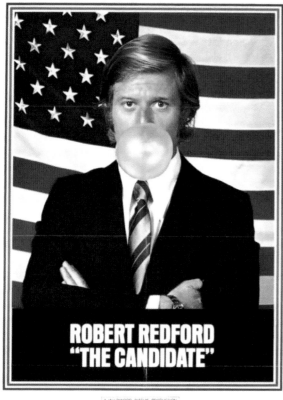

A WILDWOOD RITCHIE PRODUCTION

ROBERT REDFORD in "THE CANDIDATE" Starring PETER BOYLE and MELVYN DOUGLAS as John J. McKay Directed by MICHAEL RITCHIE
Written by JEREMY LARNER Produced by WALTER COBLENZ TECHNICOLOR® From WARNER BROS. A WARNER COMMUNICATIONS COMPANY
PG

"The Candidate" Idealistic young lawyer Bill McKay (Robert Redford), thoroughly involved with civil rights, legal aid and ecology, agrees to run for the U.S. Senate - not to win, he tells himself, but to bring vital issues before the voters. He despises political deals and compromises, but when the possibility of victory overshadows what seemed like certain defeat, his integrity begins to weaken. A fascinating and dynamic character study showing all the inner conflicts of a decent man torn between his ambition and his conscience. It tells what it costs - emotionally, morally, financially - to run for public office, and conveys all the doubts, all the self-deceptions and ultimately all the cynicism of a man who knows he has sold out for something he isn't sure he really wants. Oscar-winning screenplay by Jeremy Lardner.

Oscar Winner   Best Writing, Story and Screenplay:
                    Jeremy Larner
Box Office

Budget:$1,500,000 (estimated)

Run time 1h 50mins

Trivia

The Candidate (1972) was released a month prior to the 1972 California Presidential primary. Promotional sheets were put up in southern California resembling political posters. They had simply a photo of Robert Redford, with the slogan, "McKay: The Better Way!" - "McKay" got write-in votes in the June election.

The role of Senator Crocker Jarmon was originally offered to James Stewart, who turned the part down because he felt it was derogatory towards conservative politicians.

Groucho Marx has an uncredited walk-on cameo in what would be his last screen appearance.

A prop campaign button from this film is on display at the Smithsonian's Museum of American History in Washington. It is on display with several authentic campaign buttons.

Goofs

The red convertible driven by Marvin Lucas (Peter Boyle) has three different license plates during the opening credits: "677 EIY", "185 ENV", and "772 DYD". All are from the 1972 era in California.

At the brush fire scene, as Bill McKay exits the car to run uphill, a reporter in a yellow outfit is running behind McKay. As McKay runs approaching the firemen, the reporter in the yellow outfit is already standing beside the firemen.

When watching the anti-McKay op-ed on TV, his assistant, wearing glasses, puts his chin on his right hand, but then the shot from the front shows it with his left hand.

"Cabaret" Cambridge University student Brian Roberts arrives in Berlin in 1931 to complete his German studies. Without much money, he plans on making a living teaching English while living in an inexpensive rooming house, where he befriends another of the tenants, American Sally Bowles. She is outwardly a flamboyant, perpetually happy person who works as a singer at the decadent Kit Kat Klub, a cabaret styled venue. Sally's outward façade is matched by that of the Klub, overseen by the omnipresent Master of Ceremonies.

Sally draws Brian into her world, and initially wants him to be one of her many lovers, until she learns that he is a homosexual, albeit a celibate one. Among their other friends are his students, the poor Fritz Wendel, who wants to be a gigolo to live a comfortable life, and the straight-laced and beautiful Natalia Landauer, a Jewish heiress. Fritz initially sees Natalia as his money ticket, but eventually falls for her. However Natalia is suspect of his motives and cannot overcome their religious differences. Also into Sally and Brian's life comes the wealthy Baron Maximilian von Heune, who has the same outlook on life as Sally, but who has the money to support it.

Run time 2h 04mins

Trivia

Years before Cabaret (1972) was filmed, Liza Minnelli performed "Maybe This Time" when she appeared with her mother Judy Garland at the London Palladium.

In a 1972 interview with Dick Cavett, Liza Minnelli said that she learned Sally Bowles was a real person, so she put personal ads in newspapers in a futile attempt to meet her. Presumably Minnelli was unaware at the time that Sally Bowles wasn't her real name as the character was based on Jean Ross.

Many of the interiors of the film were done on sound stages in Munich recently vacated by the cast and crew of Willy Wonka & the Chocolate Factory (1971).

The film won 8 Oscars, though not Best Picture. It lost that as well as Best Adapted Screenplay to The Godfather (1972). As of 2020 this picture still holds the record for winning the most Oscars without winning Best Picture.

Goofs

After she's tried to seduce Brian, Sally brings her record player into his room and plays a record....this is the 1930s so the record should be spinning at 78rpm. But it isn't...it's clearly playing at 33.

When Brian thrusts the plate of cake at Sally, the cake slides off the plate and slips down to her lap. In the next shot the cake is up on her chest.

As Max drops off Brian and Sally packs for the African trip, Brian's shirt changes style and colour. In Max's car his shirt is blue with a rounded collar but, by the time he enters the apartment, it is white with a pointed collar.

"Play It Again Sam" San Francisco. After two years of marriage, Nancy Felix files for divorce from her nebbish movie journalist and film buff husband, Allan Felix. Allan receives support from his friends, married couple Dick and Linda Christie, to re-enter the dating pool, they who set him up on a series of blind dates, the four of them often double dating. Dick fits in his support for Allan while he is preoccupied with a business deal, whereas Linda's support is tinged with her own self neuroses. Non-confident with himself as a man because of Nancy's action, Allan turns to the spirit of one of his movie idols for advice on how to proceed on his dates: Humphrey Bogart, most specifically his portrayal of Rick Blaine in Casablanca (1942). In wanting those dates to work, Allan tries to be like his version of Bogey, which is nowhere close to who he really is as a person. The constant as Allan is going through this dating process is Linda, with who he can show his true colours. In the process, Allan falls in love with Linda, and he hopes she with him in return.

Box Office
Cumulative Worldwide Gross: $15,413

Run time 1h 25mins

Trivia

The set dressing and direction of a movie buff's apartment required locating many rare film posters and movie memorabilia. The value of the items ranged from as little as ten dollars to as expensive as $500. Some of the rarer pieces could only be rented by the production.

A rare instance of an America-set movie starring Woody Allen which was neither set nor shot in New York. It was shot and set in San Francisco.

Originally to be shot in Manhattan and Long Island but moved to San Francisco when New York film workers went on strike in the summer of 1971.

Hollywood legend Humphrey Bogart never actually said the phrase "Play it again, Sam" in the film Casablanca (1942) nor in any of his other movies.

Goofs

In his struggle with the hair-dryer in the bathroom, Allan knocks out half the contents of the medicine cabinet. In the next shot, the bottles he knocked out are back in the cabinet.

When Allan and Linda walk up the steps to Linda's apartment, a hand-held mike is visible at bottom of screen briefly.

While Allan is putting on his tie and talking with Bogart through the mirror, you can see a microphone wire hanging down from his shirt.

Bogart states that he shot Lizabeth Scott (in Dead Reckoning), when actually *she* shot *him.* Since he was speeding at the time, he crashed and she died.

What did happen on the Cahulawassee River?

A JOHN BOORMAN FILM Starring
JON VOIGHT · BURT REYNOLDS in "DELIVERANCE"
Co-Starring NED BEATTY · RONNY COX · Screenplay by James Dickey Based on his novel
Produced and Directed by John Boorman · PANAVISION®·TECHNICOLOR®
From Warner Bros. A Warner Communications Company
R RESTRICTED

"Deliverance". The Cahulawassee River valley in Northern Georgia is one of the last natural pristine areas of the state, which will soon change with the imminent building of a dam on the river, which in turn will flood much of the surrounding land. As such, four Atlanta city dwellers, alpha male Lewis Medlock, Ed Gentry, Bobby Trippe, and Drew Ballinger, decide to take a multi-day canoe trip on the river, with only Lewis and Ed having experience in outdoor life. They know going in that the area is isolated. Their relatively peaceful trip takes a turn for the worse halfway through with river rapids and unwelcoming locals. The four need to battle their way out of the valley and are asked to do things they never thought possible within themselves.

Box Office
Budget:$2,000,000 (estimated)
Cumulative Worldwide Gross: $4,534

Oscar nominee for : Best Picture, Best Director and Best Film Editing

Run time 1h 49mins

Trivia

Burt Reynolds broke his coccyx (tailbone) while going down the rapids when the canoe capsized. Originally, a cloth dummy was used, but it looked too fake, like a dummy going over a waterfall. While Reynolds recovered, he asked, "How did it look?" Director John Boorman replied, "Like a dummy going over a waterfall."

While filming the white water canoeing scene, Ned Beatty was thrown overboard and was sucked under by a whirlpool. A production assistant dove in to save him, but he didn't surface for thirty seconds. John Boorman asked Beatty, "How did you feel?", and Beatty responded, "I thought I was going to drown, and the first thought was, how will John finish the film without me? And my second thought was "I bet the bastard will find a way!"

According to director John Boorman, the gas station attendant's jig during "Duelling Banjos" was unscripted and spontaneous.

Burt Reynolds' breakthrough role, transforming him from a TV / B-movie actor to a film superstar.

Goofs

When the rapids get really rough, Burt Reynolds's character yells "Turn left, turn left!", and the men in the canoe steer to the right.

After killing the Toothless Man, the characters are reluctant to go to the police because his friends and family may end up on the jury. In real life, defendants are typically allowed to request a change of venue to ensure a fair trial.

When Lewis lays in the canoe, with a fractured femur, between Ed and Bobby, Lewis' position changes. One long shot only shows the two paddlers, while closer shots show Lewis' head in plain view.

In the first rapids sequence the Drew's hat disappears and reappears between shots.

"Everything you always wanted to know about sex, but were afraid to ask". In "What Is Sodomy?" married Dr. Doug Ross, who has a general practice in New York City, receives a visit from a new patient, Stavros Milos, a rural Armenian recently arrived in the US and the brother of an existing patient. The reason for Mr. Milos' visit leads to Dr. Ross questioning his own sex and love life, as well as his sanity. In "Why Do Some Women Have Trouble Reaching an Orgasm?", mod Italian couple Fabrizio and Gina have a passionate yet detached relationship, typical of what one might see in a Federico Fellini movie. The problem is that he cannot bring Gina to orgasm. In asking his friends and acquaintances how to overcome the problem, Fabrizio may come across the answer in the most inopportune of ways. In "Are Transvestites Homosexuals?" middle aged Sam, who has long been married to Tess, has been feeling out of sorts of late. At a small dinner party hosted by their daughter's in-laws, Sam takes measures to make himself feel better, being caught in his self-pleasurement which would lead to some tough questions by all. In "What Are Sex Perverts?" celebrity panellists on the game show "What's My Perversion?" ask questions of the guest to figure out what his sex perversion is.

Run time 1h 28mins

Trivia

This was the first Woody Allen movie to use for credit sequences the display font typeface of "Windsor Light Condensed", which would be regularly used on all of Allen's movies from this movie onwards.

Woody Allen interviewed Lon Chaney, Jr. for a role in this movie. This was possibly for the mad scientist role that went to John Carradine.

The film was originally banned by the Irish Film Censor in 1972, but a censored version was passed in 1979 and theatrically released in 1980.

The title's full length of thirteen words is the longest for a Woody Allen movie. Allen's second longest movie title is You Will Meet a Tall Dark Stranger (2010).

Goofs

In the final scene, The Operator says to think of baseball players to prolong sex and then says "Willie Mays, Joe Namath, Mickey Mantle". However, Joe Namath was a football player, not a baseball player.

In the "transvestite" segment, the host tells Sam the bathroom is "upstairs, first door on the left." But the bathroom door and all the other upstairs doors are on the right.

In the "sodomy" segment, the character Stavros Milos hails from Armenia. Stavros Milos is a Greek name.

At the end of the fourth segment the transvestite man's wife exclaims: "The look on their faces when the police removed your hat!" and the man laughs in response. But it was actually the man himself who had removed his hat on being recognized by his wife.

"The Getaway". Carter "Doc" McCoy is a career robber, currently in his fourth year of a ten year prison sentence at the Texas State Penitentiary. After his request for parole is denied despite he being a model prisoner, Doc, unable emotionally to endure life inside, asks his loving wife Carol McCoy to contact crooked businessman Jack Beynon, a man with political connections, to secure his release in return for he being "for sale" to Beynon. Beynon is able to get Doc released, the sale price being for Doc to plan and execute a robbery at a small bank branch in Beacon City, Texas where Beynon knows that $750,000 will be kept in the vault for the next two weeks. Rather than Doc using his own men for the job, Beynon directs that the only other people involved will be the men of his own choosing, Rudy and Frank. There are to be no casualties, which is all right with Doc who is not a murderer. After the robbery is completed and the monies divvied up accordingly, Doc and Carol will cross the border into Mexico to live out their lives away from capture. The robbery doesn't come off quite according to Doc's plan, with the result being Doc and Carol going on the run as they try to make their way into Mexico with their share of the loot.

Run time 1h 52mins

Trivia

Steve McQueen had a knack with props, especially the weapons he used in the film. Walter Hill remembered, "You can see Steve's military training in his films. He was so brisk and confident in the way he handled the guns."

In the scene where Steve McQueen and Ali MacGraw are standing outside the car and McQueen suddenly slaps her, the slap was unscripted, as can be seen by McGraw's shocked reaction.

The orange Volkswagen Beetle that Steve McQueen and Ali MacGraw pass as they flee town after the bank heist is driven by James Garner. Garner had been visiting a friend on the shoot and was hired for his vehicular skills by stunt coordinator Carey Loftin.

Sam Peckinpah shot the opening prison scenes at the Huntsville penitentiary, with Steve McQueen surrounded by actual convicts.

Goofs

After the robbery, Doc and Carol's blue car ploughs through a neighbouring porch. The windshield is clearly shattered by one of the broken porch columns. As soon as they are out of town, the blue car is immaculate.

When Rudy retrieves his gun from where Doc dropped it just before the final shoot out, he flips the empty cylinder shut without reloading it. But when he comes out the window to shoot at Doc, the gun is loaded.

After Doc and Carol arrive at the Ranch, as Doc exits the vehicle there is no one in the front seat. In the next cut, Carol is back in the passenger seat.

When Rudy, Fran and Harold are in the car, Rudy throws a paper plate and BBQ sauce gets on the windshield. But in the next shot, from inside the car, the windshield is clean.

"Sleuth". In England, the Italian English hairdresser Milo Tindle is invited by the successful writer of detective stories Andrew Wyke to visit his isolated house. The lower class Milo is the lover of Andrew's wife, who is used to have a comfortable life, and he intends to marry her. Andrew proposes Milo to steal his jewellery simulating a burglary. Milo would make a fortune selling the jewels to an intermediary; and Andrew would be reimbursed by the insurance company and would not pay alimony.

Oscar Nominees	Best Actor in a Leading Role
	Michael Caine
	Best Actor in a Leading Role
	Laurence Olivier
	Best Director
	Joseph L. Mankiewicz
	Best Music, Original Score
	John Addison

Box Office
Gross USA: $4,081,254

Run time 2h 18mins

Trivia

Michael Caine was so very much beside himself to be working with Lord Laurence Olivier that he didn't even know how to address him. Eventually, he broke down and just asked. Olivier replied "Well, I am the Lord Olivier and you are Mr. Michael Caine. Of course, that's only for the first time you address me. After that I am Larry, and you are Mike."

The reason Alan Bates thought the role was "beneath" him was that he walked out of the stage show at intermission after believing that his character had been killed when Andrew "shot" him at the end of the first act.

Michael Caine was the third choice for the part of Milo Tindle, after Albert Finney (who was deemed too plump), and Alan Bates (who turned down the role).

The laughter coming from the "dummy" Jolly Jack Tar is that of Lord Laurence Olivier.

Goofs

While Wyke is clearing the colours in the snooker game, he jumps from blue directly to black, even though the pink is on the table (in a previous shot), and in potting order comes between blue and black. Then, when the black is potted, the pink is nowhere to be seen.

When Milo throws Andrew's manuscript into the air, the Edgar Allan Poe award statuette is on the mantel; the trophy then disappears in the next shot of Andrew, only to re-emerge a few moments later.

When Milo and Andrew have blown the safe and are organizing the fake robbery, the shadows of crew members are visible behind the translucent windows.

After Inspector Doppler rings the doorbell the first time, and Andrew checks the door, the cameraman's shadow is visible on the wall before he passes the window.

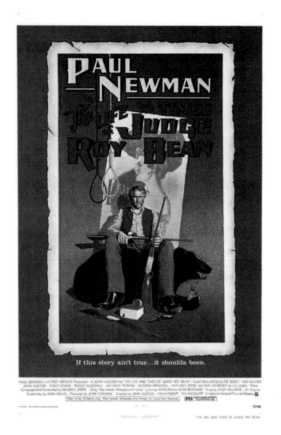

"The Life and Times of Judge Roy Bean". It's the turn of the nineteenth into twentieth centuries in Vinegaroon, Texas, west of the Rio Pecos, an area known for its general lawlessness. Due largely to an incident which nearly kills him, outlaw Roy Bean appoints himself the judge for the region, he setting up his residence and court in what was previously the saloon and whorehouse in town. He figures he has the moral authority and knowledge of the laws of Texas to become a judge in what was his flagrant disregard of those laws up to this point. He presides over court with a book of Texas statutes in front of him and his fan worship of actress Lillie Langtry in the form of large posters of her behind him. He also appoints a band of fellow outlaws as his marshals, who work solely under his direction. Standing by him through these proceedings is a young Mexican woman named Maria Elena, who saved him from that near death incident, she, in what is to look proper, living in the small shack next to the saloon instead of with him in the saloon. He becomes renowned for brandishing his form of largely illegal justice, which usually ends in the person on trial being convicted on loose judgments and hanged outside the saloon.

Run Time 2hrs

Trivia

John Milius wrote the screenplay with Lee Marvin in mind as Judge Roy Bean. He brought the script to Marvin when he was filming Pocket Money (1972), but Marvin fell asleep after one drink too many. His co-star Paul Newman found the screenplay, read it, loved it and petitioned for the part.

Anthony Perkins had led a predominantly homosexual love life up until this film. During shooting he had an affair with Victoria Principal. He later married Berry Berenson.

Although her image appears throughout the movie and her character is a prominent part of the town history, Ava Gardner does not appear in the film until approximately 15 minutes before it ends.

Paul Newman thought that Bruno the Bear stole every scene in which they appeared together, an opinion shared by some reviewers.

Goofs

When Bean regains consciousness in the alley behind the theatre, he pushes over a modern, round, galvanized garbage can.

When they bury the bear the gravestone indicates the bear was about 3 years old and died in 1899. That would mean that the visit to the town by Grizzly Adams would have occurred around 1896 or so. That would be impossible since Grizzly Adams died in 1860.

Louis XIV only had six children with Marie. And only one of those lived to adulthood. He also had 13 known illegitimate children.

Throughout the movie, the name of Ava Gardner's character is spelled Lillie Langtry. In the end credits, it is spelled Lily Langtry.

MUSIC 1972

The New Seekers	"I'd Like to Teach the World to Sing"	Polydor	8 January 1972	4
T. Rex	"Telegram Sam"	T. Rex	5 February 1972	2
Chicory Tip	"Son of My Father"	CBS	19 February 1972	3
Nilsson	"Without You"	RCA	11 March 1972	5
Royal Scots Dragoon Guards	"Amazing Grace"	RCA	15 April 1972	5
T. Rex	"Metal Guru"	EMI	20 May 1972	4
Don McLean	"Vincent"	United Artists	17 June 1972	2
Slade	"Take Me Bak 'Ome"	Polydor	1 July 1972	1
Donny Osmond	"Puppy Love"	MGM	8 July 1972	5
Alice Cooper	"School's Out"	Warner Bros.	12 August 1972	3
Rod Stewart	"You Wear It Well"	Mercury	2 September 1972	1
Slade	"Mama Weer All Crazee Now"	Polydor	9 September 1972	3
David Cassidy	"How Can I Be Sure"	Bell	30 September 1972	2
Lieutenant Pigeon	"Mouldy Old Dough"	Decca	14 October 1972	4
Gilbert O'Sullivan	"Clair"	MAM	11 November 1972	2
Chuck Berry	"My Ding-a-Ling"	Chess	25 November 1972	4
Little Jimmy Osmond	"Long Haired Lover from Liverpool"	MGM	23 December 1972	5

HEADLINES

The UK Singles Chart is the official record chart in the United Kingdom. In the 1970s, it was compiled weekly by the British Market Research Bureau (BMRB) on behalf of the British record industry with a one-week break each Christmas. Prior to 1969 many music papers compiled their own sales charts but, on 15 February 1969, the BMRB was commissioned in a joint venture by the BBC and Record Retailer to compile the chart. BMRB compiled the first chart from postal returns of sales logs from 250 record shops. The sampling cost approximately £52,000 and shops were randomly chosen and submitted figures for sales taken up to the close of trade on Saturday. The data was compiled on Monday and given to the BBC on Tuesday to be announced on Johnnie Walker's afternoon show and later published in Record Retailer (rebranded Music Week in 1972). However, the BMRB often struggled to have the full sample of sales figures returned by post. The 1971 postal strike meant that data had to be collected by telephone but this was deemed inadequate for a national chart, and by 1973 the BMRB was using motorcycle couriers to collect sales figures.

20 January – The premiere of Pink Floyd's The Dark Side of the Moon at The Dome, Brighton, is halted by technical difficulties. The Dark Side of the Moon would be played in its entirety the following night, but it would be a full year before the album was released.

21 January - Keith Richards jumps on stage to jam with Chuck Berry at the Hollywood Palladium, but is ordered off for playing too loud. Berry later claims that he did not recognize Keith and would not have booted him if he did.

9 February – Paul McCartney's new band, Wings, make their live debut at the University of Nottingham. It is McCartney's first public concert since The Beatles' 1966 US tour.

13 February – Led Zeppelin's concert in Singapore is cancelled when government officials will not let them off the airplane because of their long hair.

19 February - Paul McCartney's single "Give Ireland Back to the Irish" (which was inspired by the "Bloody Sunday" massacre in Ireland on 30 January 1972) is banned by the BBC.

25 March – The 17th Eurovision Song Contest is held in the Usher Hall, Edinburgh, Scotland. The only time (as of 2012) Scotland hosted the contest.

16 April – Electric Light Orchestra make their live debut at the Fox and Greyhound pub in Park Lane, Croydon, England.

2 May – Stone the Crows lead guitarist Les Harvey is electrocuted on stage during a show in Swansea, Wales, by touching a poorly connected microphone. Harvey died in a hospital a few hours later. The band's lead singer, Maggie Bell, Harvey's long-time girlfriend, was also hospitalized, having collapsed on stage after the incident.

1 June - Premiere of Harrison Birtwistle's The Triumph of Time in London.

12 July - First performance of Peter Maxwell Davies's opera Taverner at the Royal Opera House.

8 October - David Hughes is taken ill while singing the role of Pinkerton in Madam Butterfly in London. He completes the performance but dies shortly afterwards of heart failure.

The New Seekers

" I'd Like to Teach the World to Sing (In Perfect Harmony)"

"I'd Like to Teach the World to Sing (In Perfect Harmony)" is a pop song that originated as the jingle "Buy the World a Coke" in the ground breaking 1971 "Hilltop" television commercial for Coca-Cola and sung by The Hillside Singers. "Buy the World a Coke" was produced by Billy Davis and portrayed a positive message of hope and love, featuring a multicultural collection of teenagers on top of a hill appearing to sing the song.

The popularity of the jingle led to it being re-recorded in two versions; one by The New Seekers and another by The Hillside Singers, as a full-length song, dropping references to Coca-Cola. The song became a hit record in the US and the UK.

T Rex

"Telegram Sam"

"Telegram Sam" is a song written by Marc Bolan for the British rock group T. Rex, appearing on their 1972 album The Slider. The song was their third UK number one single, remaining at the top of the charts for two weeks before being knocked off the top by "Son of My Father" by Chicory Tip. "Telegram Sam" was the first single to be issued by Marc Bolan's own T.Rex Wax Co. label, and was released on 21st January 1972. The B-side featured two songs in the UK, "Cadilac" (as printed on the EMI label of the original single) and "Baby Strange", the latter also included in the album The Slider. "Telegram Sam" was written by Bolan about his manager Tony Secunda (Telegram Sam = Tony Secunda) who was his 'main man' in respect of him being Bolan's manager and narcotics supplier.

The single was recorded at the Rosenberg Studios in Copenhagen, Denmark in November 1971.

Chicory Tip

"Son Of My Father"

"Son of My Father" is a song popularised in 1972 by Chicory Tip. A copy of Giorgio's version found its way to studio manager Roger Easterby who then persuaded the British band Chicory Tip to record it. The song, produced by Easterby and Des Champ, was recorded on Christmas Eve 1971 in the studio of George Martin. The song is notable as the first UK number one single to prominently feature a synthesizer, in this case a Moog synthesizer, programmed by Chris Thomas. The B side of the single is "Pride Comes Before A Fall". The song reached No. 1 on the UK Singles Chart for three weeks in February 1972.

The band released the song in the US under the shortened name Chicory, but it only reached No. 91 on the Billboard Hot 100Since its release, the tune of the chorus of "Son of My Father" has been regularly used on the terraces of British football grounds for football chants.

Badfinger

"Without You"

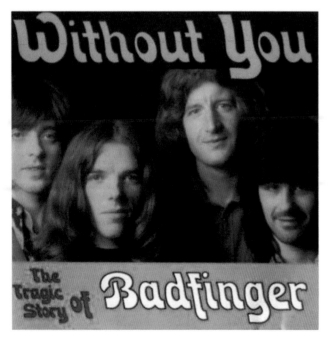

"Without You" is a song written by Pete Ham and Tom Evans of British rock group Badfinger, and first released on their 1970 album No Dice. The power ballad has been recorded by over 180 artists, and versions released as singles by Harry Nilsson (1971) and Mariah Carey (1994) became international best-sellers. Paul McCartney once described the ballad as "the killer song of all time". In 1972, writers Ham and Evans received the British Academy's Ivor Novello Award for Best Song Musically and Lyrically. The two writers of the song, Ham and Evans, later committed suicide due to legal and financial issues. In Evans' case, it was a dispute over song writing royalties for "Without You" that precipitated his action. Song writing royalties had become the subject of constant legal wrangling for Evans, and in 1983, following an acrimonious argument with his bandmate Joey Molland over the royalties for the song, Evans hanged himself.

The Royal Scots Dragoon Guards

"Amazing Grace"

"**Amazing Grace**" Although Judy Collins used it as a catharsis for her opposition to the Vietnam War, two years after her rendition, the Royal Scots Dragoon Guards, senior Scottish regiment of the British Army, recorded an instrumental version featuring a bagpipe soloist accompanied by a pipe band. The tempo of their arrangement was slowed to allow for the bagpipes, but it was based on Collins'.

The Royal Scots Dragoon Guards started performing in competitions, concerts and parades. It was the first official organized pipes and drums in the history of the regiment. Their most famous piece is "Amazing Grace", which reached number one in the charts in the United Kingdom.
The track sold over seven million copies by mid-1977, and was awarded a gold disc.

T Rex

" Metal Guru "

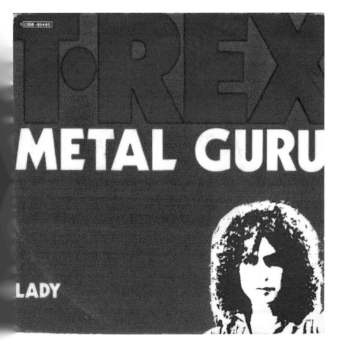

"**Metal Guru**" is a song by the British rock band T. Rex, written by Marc Bolan. It was the band's fourth (and final) number one on the UK Singles Chart when it topped the chart for four weeks from May–June 1972. It was also included on the album The Slider in 1972. Despite coming only ten months after the success of "Get It On", it failed to chart in the United States. The song reached No. 45 in Canada in July 1972. Bolan himself described the song's apparent religious references as this:

"Is a festival of life song" I relate 'Metal Guru' to all Gods around. I believe in a God, but I have no religion. With 'Metal Guru', it's like someone special, it must be a Godhead. I thought how God would be; he'd be all alone without a telephone. I don't answer the phone any more. I have codes where people ring me at certain times."

Don Mclean

"Vincent"

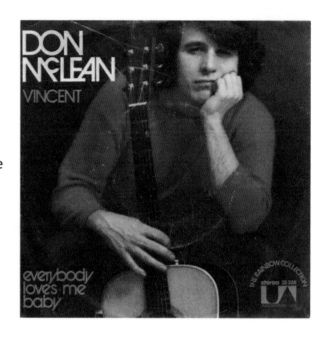

"**Vincent**" is a song by Don McLean written as a tribute to Vincent van Gogh. It is often erroneously titled after its opening refrain, "Starry Starry Night", a reference to Van Gogh's 1889 painting The Starry Night.

McLean wrote the lyrics in 1971 after reading a book about the life of Van Gogh. It was released on McLean's 1971 American Pie album, and the following year the song became the No. 1 hit in the UK Singles Chart for two weeks, and No. 12 in the United States, where it also hit No. 2 on the Easy Listening chart. Billboard ranked it as the No. 94 song for 1972.

The song makes use mainly of the guitar but also includes the accordion, marimba, and strings.

Slade

"Get It Oh"

"**Take Me Bak 'Ome**" is a song by the British rock band Slade, released in 1972 as a non-album single. It was written by lead vocalist Noddy Holder and bassist Jim Lea, and produced by Chas Chandler. It reached No. 1 in the UK, giving the band their second number one single, and remained in the charts for thirteen weeks. The song was certified UK Silver by BPI in 1972.

In the United States, the song reached No. 97. The song would be included on the band's 1973 compilation album Sladest. Shortly after the single's release, Slade played at the Great Western Festival near Lincoln. Before their performance, the band had fears over whether or not they could win over the 50,000-strong crowd. Now deemed a 'pop band', the announcement of their imminent appearance on the stage was met with outbreaks of booing from the audience.

Donny Osmond

"Puppy Love"

"Puppy Love" is a popular song written by Paul Anka in 1960 for Annette Funicello. Twelve years later the song was revived by Donny Osmond. It was released on February 19, 1972, and reached No. 3 on the Billboard Hot 100 on the 1st April 1972. It peaked at No. 1 in April 1972 on both the Canadian RPM singles chart for three weeks and the UK Singles Chart for five weeks the following July. Billboard ranked this version as the No. 67 song for 1972. It was certified Gold by the RIAA on 24th March 1972. The song was also covered by British pop group S Club Juniors in 2002. On 15th March 1972, DJ Robert W. Morgan played the Donny Osmond version for 90 minutes straight on KHJ in Los Angeles.

After receiving numerous calls from listeners, LAPD raided the station studios. Confused, the officers left without making any arrests.

Alice Cooper

"Schools Out"

"Schools Out" became Alice Cooper's first major hit single, reaching #7 on the Billboard Hot 100 pop singles chart and propelling the album to #2 on the Billboard 200 pop albums chart. It was the highest-charting single for the Alice Cooper band, and its #7 peak position was matched only by "Poison" among Cooper's solo efforts.

Billboard ranked it as the No. 75 song for 1972. In Canada, the single went to #3 on the RPM Top Singles Chart following the album reaching #1.

In Britain, the song went to #1 on the UK Singles Chart for three weeks in August 1972. It also marked the first time that Alice Cooper became regarded as more than just a theatrical novelty act.

Rod Stewart

"You Wear It Well"

"You Wear It Well" is a song written by Rod Stewart and Martin Quittenton, performed by Stewart. It uses an arrangement markedly similar to that of "Maggie May", one of Stewart's hits from the previous year.

Stewart recorded "You Wear It Well" for the 1972 album Never a Dull Moment, and released it as a single on 12th August. The song became an international hit, reaching number one on the UK Singles Chart. In the US, "You Wear It Well" peaked at number 13 on the Billboard Hot 100 chart.

Stewart performed the song live on BBC's Top of the Pops with the full line-up of Faces, along with Quittenton on classical guitar and Dick "Tricky Dicky" Powell on fiddle joining them.

Slade

"Mama Weer All Crazee Now"

"Mama Weer All Crazee Now" is a song by the British rock band Slade, released in 1972 as the lead single from their third studio album Slayed? It was written by lead vocalist Noddy Holder and bassist Jim Lea, and produced by Chas Chandler. It reached No. 1 in the UK, giving the band their third number one single, and remained in the charts for ten weeks. "Mama Weer All Crazee Now" was the first tune Lea wrote entirely on his own. Holder got the idea for the lyrics at the band's concert at Wembley Arena in London. After the show, he looked at the remains of the auditorium's smashed seating and thought "Christ, everyone must have been crazy tonight." The song was originally titled "My My We're All Crazy Now". When Holder and Lea played the song acoustically to Chandler for the first time, he thought Holder was singing "Mama We're All Crazy Now". The name was then changed accordingly as Holder and Lea felt Chandler's title was better.

David Cassidy

"How Can I Be Sure"

"How Can I Be Sure" was recorded for the album Rock Me Baby by David Cassidy.

In the British Isles "How Can I Be Sure" would afford Cassidy a #1 hit on both the Irish Singles Chart and also (for two weeks) the singles chart for the UK, being the second of Cassidy's overall 11 UK chart hits six of which would reach the Top Ten including his second #1 UK hit: the double A-side hit "Daydreamer"/"The Puppy Song" (#1 for three weeks in 1973).

"How Can I Be Sure" also charted with more moderate impact in Australia (#16), Canada (#22), Germany (#33), and the Netherlands (#13).

Lieutenant Pigeon

"Mouldy Old Dough"

"Mouldy Old Dough" is an instrumental single, which was a hit for Lieutenant Pigeon. It was written by Nigel Fletcher and Rob Woodward and first produced by them under the name of their other band, Stavely Makepeace. Recorded in the front room of Woodward's Coventry semi-detached house, it featured his mother Hilda Woodward on piano, in a boogie-woogie, honky-tonk, ragtime style. The only lyrics are the growled title "Mouldy Old Dough" and "Dirty Old Man" by Fletcher. When Fletcher asked what they meant, their author, Rob Woodward, said he had no idea.

Despite initial disapproval from their long-term manager and friend, David Whitehouse, they went ahead with its release. It is the only British number one single to feature a mother and son.

Gilbert O'Sullivan

"Clair"

"**Clair**" is a song by Gilbert O'Sullivan, released in 1972 as the first single from his second album Back to Front. It was written by O'Sullivan and produced by Gordon Mills, and is one of O'Sullivan's biggest-selling singles. The song is the love song of a close family friend who babysits a young girl (actually the artist's manager's daughter); though for the first part of the song, the ambiguous text leads one to think that it is from one adult to another. "Clair" was the number one single on the UK Singles Chart for two weeks in November 1972, and number one in Canada on the RPM 100 singles chart. In late December, it peaked at number two on the Billboard Hot 100 in the US, behind both "Me and Mrs. Jones" by Billy Paul and "You're So Vain" by Carly Simon. "Clair" was also O'Sullivan's second and last number one hit on the U.S. Easy Listening chart, after "Alone Again.

Chuck Berry

"My Ding-a-Ling"

"**My Ding-a-Ling**" is a novelty song written and recorded by Dave Bartholomew. It was covered by Chuck Berry in 1972 and became his only number-one Billboard Hot 100 single in the United States. Later that year, in a longer unedited form, it was included on the album The London Chuck Berry Sessions. "My Ding-a-Ling" was originally recorded by Dave Bartholomew in 1952 for King Records. When Bartholomew moved to Imperial Records, he re-recorded the song under the new title, "Little Girl Sing Ting-a-Ling". In 1954, the Bees on Imperial released a version entitled "Toy Bell." Doug Clark and the Hot Nuts recorded it in 1961.

The lyrics with their sly tone and innuendo (and the enthusiasm of Berry and the audience) caused many radio stations to refuse to play it. British morality campaigner Mary Whitehouse tried unsuccessfully to get the song banned.

Jimmy Osmand

"Long Haired Lover From Liverpool"

"Long Haired Lover from Liverpool" is a pop song best known as a hit for Little Jimmy Osmond. Written by Christopher Kingsley (somehow credited as Christopher Dowden on the UK release) and produced by Mike Curb and Perry Botkin Jr, "Long Haired Lover from Liverpool" was a UK number one single for Jimmy Osmond. Riding high on the popularity of the Osmond's, Jimmy (the youngest sibling) had a massive hit with the song, in the process becoming the youngest person to ever reach number one on the UK Singles Chart aged 9 years 8 months.

A UK number one for five weeks in December 1972, it was the Christmas number one that year, and has since sold over a million copies in the UK. It also reached number two on the Australian Singles Chart and number 38 on the US, Billboard Hot 100.

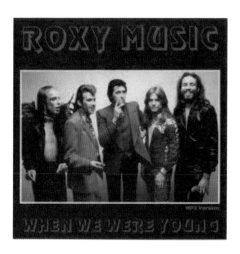

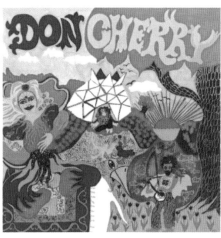

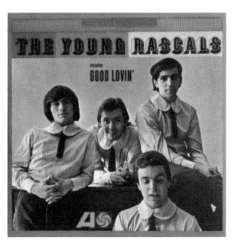

61

WORLD EVENTS 1972

January

1st   Kurt Waldheim of Austria became the fourth Secretary General of the United Nations, succeeding U Thant. Waldheim served two five-year terms. It would only be after he became President of Austria in 1986 that the world would learn that Waldheim had been a Nazi officer being investigated by the UN War Crimes Commission.

2nd   Juliane Koepcke, the sole survivor of the Christmas Eve crash of LANSA Flight 508, was found alive by three hunters deep inside the Amazon jungle in Peru. The only survivor of 93 persons on the plane, she had followed a stream for nine days until finding help.

4th   The first scientific electronic pocket calculator, the HP-35 was introduced by Hewlett-Packard and priced at $395 (equivalent to more than $2,400 in 2019). Although hand-held electronic machines that could multiply and divide (such as the Canon Pocketronic) had been made since 1971, the HP-35 could handle higher functions including logarithms and trigonometry.

5th   From his "Western White House" residence in San Clemente, California, President Richard Nixon announced that the United States would develop the space shuttle as the next phase of the American space program, with 5.5 billion dollars allocated to the first reusable spacecraft. "It would transform the space frontier of the 1970s into familiar territory," said Nixon, "easily accessible for human endeavour of the 1980s and 1990s."

7th   Police located and defused time bombs that had been placed in safe deposit boxes in eight banks in New York, Chicago and San Francisco in July 1971. The bombs, described in an anonymous letter, sent the day before, each had a "seven-month fuse" and would have exploded in February. A ninth bomb had gone off prematurely in September.

11th   Bill France, Jr. succeeded his father as President of the National Association for Stock Car Auto Racing NASCAR. Over the next 28 years, France oversaw the growth of stock car racing to a multibillion-dollar industry and one of the most popular sports in the United States.

13th   A plane, taking West Germany's Chancellor Willy Brandt home after his visit to the United States, came within 500 feet of colliding with Eastern Airlines Flight 870, as both planes were flying at 33,000 feet 85 miles northeast of Jacksonville, Florida. A spokesman for the Professional Air Traffic Controllers' Association said on 15th January that the incident had been reported to him by controllers at the Jacksonville airport.

15th   At 3:00 pm, at the balcony of the Christiansborg Palace in Copenhagen, Prime Minister Jens Otto Krag proclaimed three times, "King Frederik IX is dead! Long live Her Majesty Queen Margrethe II!" With that, Margrethe became the second queen of Denmark, with the same name as her ancestor, who had reigned from 1353 to 1412. There is no provision for a coronation, or even a crown, for the monarchs of Denmark.

18th   The United States Coast Guard cutter Storis seized two Soviet fishing vessels, the flagship Lamut and the sterntrawler Kolyvan, after they had penetrated American territorial waters less than 12 miles of the Alaskan coast. The ships were detained at the Adak Naval Air Station until 17th February then released after the Soviets paid a $250,000 fine.

January

20th | In Geneva, the member nations of the Organization of the Petroleum Exporting Countries (OPEC) agreed to raise their price for crude oil by 8.49 percent, to $2.49 per barrel, the first of many sharp increases that would follow.

21st | India added three new States, bringing the total to 20, with statehood granted to Tripura, Manipur and Meghalaya. On the same day, Mizoram and Arunachal Pradesh were granted union territory status (both granted statehood in 1987). As of 2009, there are 28 states and seven territories in India.

25th | In a nationally televised address, President Nixon revealed that Henry Kissinger had been secretly negotiating with North Vietnamese leaders, and announced "a plan for peace that can end the war in Vietnam". North Vietnam rejected the proposal the next day.

26th | On the lawn in front of the Australian Parliament in Canberra, four young Aborigine men (Michael Anderson, Billy Craigie, Gary Williams and Tony Coorey) erected a tent that they called the Aboriginal Embassy, a symbol of the feeling that the indigenous Australians were treated as foreigners in their own homeland. Soon, the four were joined by others, until nearly 2,000 supporters encamped in front of the Parliament. The "embassy" was torn down six months later.

27th | The first home video game system, Odyssey, was introduced by Magnavox. Designed by Ralph Baer, the console could be hooked up to a television set for two players to play a tennis-like game, similar to Nolan Bushnell's game Pong.

February

1st | Four days after Nazi hunter Beate Klarsfeld had found that Klaus Barbie was living in Bolivia (as "Klaus Altmann"), the French government requested his extradition. Barbie was not brought to justice until 1983.

3rd | The 1972 Winter Olympics opened in Sapporo, Japan, with 1,006 athletes from 35 nations marching in the opening ceremony at Makomanai Stadium. Schoolboy Hideki Takada lit the Olympic flame.

4th | Argentina's worst serial killer, Carlos Robledo Puch, was captured after committing 11 murders in less than a year.

7th | Keith Holyoake resigned as Prime Minister of New Zealand after more than 11 years. He was replaced by the Deputy Prime Minister, Jack Marshall, who would lead the government until elections held on 25th November.

9th | The Iran blizzard ended after seven days, during which as much as 26 feet (7.9 m) of snow buried villages in north western, central and southern Iran. An estimated 4,000 people were killed, particularly in the area around Ardakan.

10th | Kinney Services, Inc., a conglomerate which had purchased the Warner Bros. studio in 1969, completed reorganization as shareholders approved its disincorporation in New York and its reincorporation in Delaware, with the new name of Warner Communications, Inc. The company, which now owns Turner Broadcasting, HBO, Cinemax, DC Comics, New Line Cinema, ViacomCBS and part of TheCW television network, is now known as WarnerMedia.

13th | The 1972 Winter Olympics closed in Sapporo. The Soviet Union had the most medals (16) and most gold medals (8), followed by East Germany, Switzerland, the Netherlands, and the United States.

14th | The animated TV special The Lorax by Dr. Seuss first aired on CBS.

15th | The United States granted copyright protection, for the first time, to sound recordings. Previously, only the written musical and lyrical compositions could be protected from reproduction.

17th | The Volkswagen Beetle broke the record for the most popular automobile in history, as the 15,007,034th Beetle was produced. Between 1908 and 26th May 1927, a total of 15,007,033 Model T's had been produced.

19th | The TV show All in the Family first aired what became its most famous episode, which ended with black musician Sammy Davis, Jr. giving a kiss on the cheek to America's most popular bigot, Archie Bunker.

21st | At 11:30 a.m. local time (0330 UTC) in Peking (now Beijing), Richard M. Nixon became the first President of the United States to visit the People's Republic of China, ending more than 22 years of hostility between the two nations. Nixon greeted China's Prime Minister Zhou Enlai with one of the most famous handshakes in history. "When our hands met", Nixon would write later, "one era ended and another began", while Zhou told Nixon on their trip from the airport, "Your handshake came over the vastest ocean in the world – twenty-five years of no communication."

24th | Twenty-eight men on board the Soviet nuclear submarine K-19 were killed when fires broke out in three of its compartments while the sub was submerged. The twelve survivors remained trapped inside the sub as it was towed, over the next three weeks, from the Arctic Ocean back to the Kola Peninsula.

26th | The Buffalo Creek flood killed 125 people in Logan County, West Virginia, after a coal slurry impoundment dam gave way at 8:05 a.m., during heavy rains. Over the next several minutes, 132 million US gallons (500,000 cubic metres; 500 million litres) of coal waste and water in a wave over the communities in its path.

29th | "We now have evidence that the settlement of the Nixon administration's biggest antitrust case was privately arranged between Atty. Gen. John Mitchell and the top lobbyist for the company involved", was the opener to Jack Anderson's syndicated column. "We have this on the word of the lobbyist herself, crusty, capable Dita Beard of the International Telephone and Telegraph Co. She acknowledged the secret deal after we obtained a highly incriminating memo, written by her, from ITT's files." The subsequent investigation by the Nixon Administration into the source of leaked information was one of seven improper activities cited by the Watergate Committee in its final report.

March

2ⁿᵈ Pioneer 10 was launched from the Cape Kennedy at 8:49 p.m. Bearing a 6-by-9-inch gold anodized plaque that contained a message for alien civilizations; the American probe attained a record speed of more than 30,000 m.p.h. on its way to the planet Jupiter, which it would reach on 3ʳᵈ December 1973. Pioneer 10 became, on 13ᵗʰ June 1983, the first man-made object to depart the solar system, moving toward the star Aldebaran. The last transmissions from Pioneer 10 were received on 31ˢᵗ March 1997, and the last signal was received on 22ⁿᵈ January 2003.

4ᵗʰ "About 1.1 million young people reached adulthood at midnight", as the New York Times described it, when a law took effect in California to lower the age of majority from 21 to 18.

7ᵗʰ TWA Flight 7 was half an hour into its flight from New York to Los Angeles when the airline's officials were notified that it had a time bomb on board. The plane landed back at JFK at 12:10 pm. A trained German shepherd named "Brandy" sniffed out the explosive, found in an attaché case in the cockpit. With five pounds of C4, the device would have destroyed the Boeing 707, with 52 on board; in mid-flight at 1:00 pm. Police defused the explosive with 12 minutes to spare.

8ᵗʰ The highest recorded speed for a gust of wind was measured at 207 m.p.h. during a storm at Thule Air Base in Greenland.

11ᵗʰ Carnival Cruise Lines made its very first voyage, as the Mardi Gras departed Miami for an 8-day cruise ... and ran aground on a sandbar. The 530 passengers, most of whom were travel agents and their families, continued to enjoy themselves until tugboats dislodged the ship the next day, and the new company received national publicity from the incident.

March

12th | The European satellite TD-1A was launched, designed to be the first to measure the ultraviolet spectrum.

15th | The Godfather, directed by Francis Ford Coppola, debuted in five cinemas in New York City, and would set a record (which stood until 1975) for the highest-grossing film in history, taking in $87,500,000 in its first release.

20th | Twenty-four mountaineers were killed by an avalanche on Japan's Mount Fuji, and another six were missing and presumed dead.

23rd | The first media event surrounding the recently discovered, cave-dwelling Tasaday people took place in the Philippines as reporters, scientists, and VIPs (including Charles Lindbergh) were brought in by helicopter to meet a group of people who had never made it out of the Stone Age. It was not until after the 1986 overthrow of Philippine President Ferdinand Marcos that it was discovered that the 26 Tasaday "cavemen" had been ordinary people going along with a hoax.

25th | The 254th and last original episode of the TV series Bewitched was broadcast, ending a run that had started on 17th September 1964.

29th | For the first time since 1966, authorities in East Germany opened the Berlin Wall for an eight-day period in order to allow visitors from West Germany during the Easter holidays, and tens of thousands of Westerners received permission to travel to East Berlin. For the first time since 1952, the Communist government permitted visitors to go beyond the capital and into the countryside as well. The visits were permitted until 5th April.

April

3rd | Silent film legend Charlie Chaplin returned to the United States after more than 20 years of self-imposed exile. "The Little Tramp", now 82, had been invited back for the Academy Awards.

6th | In response to the invasion of South Vietnam by troops from the north, more than 400 American airplanes bombed North Vietnam in the heaviest attacks there since 1968.

7th | WBC titleholder Bob Foster knocked out WBA champ Vicente Rondon with five seconds left in the second round of their match at Miami Beach, to become the undisputed light heavyweight boxing champion of the world.

13th | The first destruction of an enemy tank by Cobra attack helicopter was made by CW2 Barry McIntyre, in the course of the Battle of An Loc. The manoeuvrable and destructive Cobras were able to stop entire columns of North Vietnamese tanks, and turned the course of the Easter Offensive.

17th | The Ford Motor Company announced the recall of all of its 1972 model year Ford Torino and Mercury Montego automobiles—436,000 cars in all—to correct a defect in the rear axles. The following week, the company ordered a second recall of the vehicles for further repairs.

19th | Four American warships were attacked by three MiG-17 jets from North Vietnam. The destroyers USS Higbee and Lloyd Thomas, the guided missile frigate USS Sterett, and the light cruiser USS Oklahoma City were attacked, with the Higbee having a gun mount destroyed by a 250 kg bomb, and four sailors wounded.

April

21st | Sweden passed the world's first law officially recognizing change of gender, with the amendment, effective from 1st July off civil registration rules to accommodate change of birth registrations for individuals who had undergone, or applied to have, sex change surgery.

23rd | In a referendum in France, voters approved the treaty adding Britain, Ireland and Denmark into the Common Market, with more than 68% in favour.

25th | Photographs that developed "right before your eyes" were introduced when Edwin H. Land of the Polaroid Corporation demonstrated the SX-70 film and camera.

 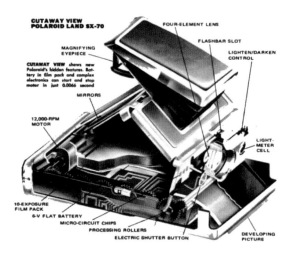

26th | The Lockheed L-1011, a competitor to the Boeing 747 and the DC-10, was introduced, with Eastern Airlines purchasing the first of the new jets.

28th | An astronomer with the Lawrence Livermore National Laboratory announced the possible discovery of a tenth planet. Joseph L. Brady, relying on computer calculations of gravitational data, said that the planet would be larger than Saturn and more than five billion miles from the Sun. The possibility was ruled out after further study.

May

2nd | U.S. Patent 3,659,915 was issued to Corning Glass, the first ever for fibre optic cable.

3rd | Les Harvey, 27, guitarist of Stone the Crows, was fatally electrocuted before a crowd of 1,200 people, as he was preparing to perform at the Top Rank ballroom at Swansea University in Wales. Reportedly, Harvey's hands were wet when he took hold of a microphone that was not properly grounded.

7th | Edmund Kemper, 23, picked up two hitchhiking Fresno State University students, roommates Mary Anne Pesce and Anita Luchessa, drove them to a remote location, murdered them, and then dismembered their bodies. It was the start of a nearly year-long crime spree as a serial killer. Prior to murdering his six randomly picked victims, Kemper had killed his grandparents when he was 15 and spent several years in juvenile detention before being released from a psychiatric hospital. Kemper's last two victims were his mother and her friend, after which he called the Santa Cruz police.

11th | Rogers C. B. Morton, the United States Secretary of the Interior, announced that construction would begin of the controversial trans-Alaska oil pipeline.

May

13th | The first successful use of the laser-guided bomb was accomplished when the Thanh Hóa Bridge was destroyed in North Vietnam, "accomplishing in a single mission what seven years of non-precision bombing had failed to do". The United States had first bombed the 540-foot-long (160 m) concrete and steel structure in 1965. Twelve F-4 fighters made runs with fifteen Mark 84 and nine Mark 118 bombs to render the structure useless.

16th | The first financial derivatives exchange, the International Monetary Market (IMM), opened on the Chicago Mercantile Exchange. With greater fluctuation of currency exchange rates, the IMM opened a new era in trading by allowing purchase of futures on three currencies. The first trades were for the British pound, the Deutschmark, and the Japanese yen.

18th | An Antonov An-10 turboprop airplane with 108 persons aboard crashed while attempting an emergency landing at Kharkov. A one-paragraph announcement of the accident was printed in the Soviet newspaper Pravda two days later, noting that "The passengers and crew were killed. A government commission has been appointed for inquiry into the causes of the disaster."

20th | Professional golfer Jane Blalock was disqualified from the Bluegrass Invitational for not marking her ball properly, and then failing to take a two-stroke penalty. Within a month, the LPGA Tour would move to suspend Blalock. In response, she would file an anti-trust lawsuit against the LPGA. The Jane Blalock cheating controversy would continue until 1975, when both parties agreed to settle their claims against one another.

24th | West Germany formally relinquished all claims to eastern territories lost by Germany to the USSR and to Poland following World War II, as the West German President Gustav Heinemann signed the Moscow Treaty and Warsaw Treaty. The treaties had been approved the week before by the Bundestag and the Bundesrat. Included were the formerly German city of Königsberg, which became Russian Kaliningrad, and the former Breslau, which became Wrocław in Poland.

28th | The first major accident, resulting from the design of the Ford Pinto automobile, happened near Barstow, California. Mrs. Lilly Gray and her teenage son, Richard Grimshaw, were severely burned after the gas tank in their 1972 Pinto exploded after the car stalled and was rear-ended on Interstate Highway 15. Mrs. Gray died of her injuries, and her son was scarred for life. A jury awarded $125 million in punitive damages, against Ford Motor, to the family, which was reduced to $3.5 million, and more than $3 million in compensatory damages. The verdict was upheld on appeal in 1981 in the landmark case of Gray v. Ford Motor Company, 119 Cal. App.3d 757.

31st | The 145th and final mission of the CORONA spy satellite program came to an end when its exposed film was recovered. Since 1959, the Corona satellites were launched with Kodak film, and then returned to Earth after taking photos over the Soviet Union and its neighbours. Transmission of images from spy satellites made the Corona program obsolete.

June

1st | Pablo Picasso completed his final painting, The Embrace, at his home in Mougins, France. He died ten months later at the age of 91.

3rd | Sally Priesand became the first American woman to be ordained as a rabbi, as one of 26 Hebrew Union College graduates ordained at the Isaac M. Wise Temple in Cincinnati.

June

6th	U.S. Patent No. 3,668,658 was granted to the IBM Corporation for the first "floppy disk" (officially, "diskettes" for the IBM 3330 computer).

6th U.S. Patent No. 3,668,658 was granted to the IBM Corporation for the first "floppy disk" (officially, "diskettes" for the IBM 3330 computer).

7th The 1950s nostalgia musical Grease began the first of 3,388 performances on Broadway, running until 13th April 1980.

9th At 10:45 p.m., the Canyon Lake Dam at Rapid City, South Dakota, gave way under the pressure of a downpour, sending millions of gallons of water through the city. The results of the Black Hills flood were 238 people killed, and 3,057 more injured. More than 5,000 vehicles and 700 homes were destroyed, and the total damages were $165 million.

12th American Airlines Flight 96 made an emergency landing after an improperly closed cargo door was blown off at 12,500 feet, shortly after the DC-10 took off from Detroit for a flight to Buffalo. Captain Bryce McCormick struggled with failing flight controls to land the jet, and the 67 people on board, at Cleveland. A similar accident in 1974 on a Turkish Airlines Flight 981, all 346 people on board were killed after the cargo door fell off.

15th Dougal Robertson, his wife, three children, and a family friend, were sailing on their yacht Lucette, when the boat was attacked and sunk by orca whales. The six survived 38 days adrift in the Pacific Ocean, then on an inflatable life raft, then on a dinghy. Robertson wrote about the experience in a book, Survive the Savage Sea, later made into a 1991 film.

16th A rock fall, inside a mile-long railway tunnel near Soissons, France, led to the collision and derailment of two passenger trains, killing 107 people. At 8:50 p.m., six carloads of passengers were traveling from Paris to Laon, and after entering the tunnel, ran into a pile of rock and concrete. Minutes later, as survivors lay in the wreckage; a second train came into the tunnel, from the opposite direction, with its own three carloads of passengers, colliding with the rubble and the first train. There were 90 persons who survived their injuries.

18th In the worst air disaster in Britain up to that time, all 118 persons aboard British European Airways Flight 548 were killed when the Trident jetliner crashed at 5:29 p.m., shortly after take-off from Heathrow.

21st The world record for highest altitude in a helicopter (40,814 ft or 12,440 m) was set by Jean Boulet in an Aerospatiale SA-315 Lama. Boulet said that "that flight also wound up being the longest autoration in history because the turbine died as soon as I reduced power."

22nd The 1,000,000th Ford Thunderbird was produced, rolling off of an assembly line in Los Angeles. The car was first produced in 1955.

26th Boxer Roberto Duran defeated WBA lightweight champion Ken Buchanan in a fight at New York's Madison Square Garden, beginning a 17-year reign in boxing at the levels of lightweight (1972–79), welterweight (1980), junior middleweight (1983) and middleweight (1989).

27th Nolan Bushnell and Ted Dabney incorporated Atari, Inc. in California, to mass-produce video game machines. Their first choice of name, "Syzygy", was already in use by a candle maker in Mendocino, so the entrepreneurs used a term from Japanese gaming.

July

2nd | The musical Fiddler on the Roof closed on Broadway after a record 3,242 performances. With music by Jerry Bock and lyrics by Sheldon Harnick, Fiddler had first been performed on 22nd September 1964.

3rd | Prime Minister of India Indira Gandhi and President of Pakistan Zulfikar Ali Bhutto signed the Simla Agreement, resolving to peacefully negotiate future disputes, releasing prisoners of war, and withdrawing their military forces behind their sides of a 460-mile long border.

6th | The first payment of "hush money", via the Committee to Re-Elect the President, to the Watergate burglars, was made. Over eight months, lasting until 22nd March 1973, almost $430,000 was paid to the men to keep them from implicating the White House in the break-in of DNC headquarters.

10th | An intentionally set fire on board the aircraft carrier USS Forrestal as it sat in port in Norfolk, Virginia, caused USD $7,000,000 worth of damage, and was the largest single act of sabotage in United States Navy history. Seaman apprentice Jeffrey Allison was later convicted of having started the blaze. The Forrestal had been the site of a fire in 1967 that had killed 132 persons.

11th | The long anticipated chess match between world champion Boris Spassky of the Soviet Union, and United States champion Bobby Fischer, began in Iceland at Reykjavík, nine days and seven minutes after the original start date. With no opponent present, Spassky made his opening move at 5:00 pm by moving his queen's pawn forward two spaces in the first of 24 games. Fischer walked into the 2,500 seat Reykjavík Sports Hall minutes later.

Boris Spassky

Bobby Fischer

15th | Actress Jane Fonda posed for photographs at a North Vietnamese anti-aircraft gun at Hanoi, and the first images were printed in a newspaper in Poland. Pictures of the actress, gazing through the gunsight of a weapon used to shoot down American planes during the ongoing Vietnam War, ran worldwide the next day.

17th | The American destroyer USS Warrington was damaged beyond repair by two underwater explosions while in the Gulf of Tonkin. The blasts were believed to have been caused by American mines that had washed away after having been laid in North Vietnam's ports. The Warrington became the only American warship to be lost in the Vietnam War.

July

19th The guided missile frigate USS Biddle was attacked by five North Vietnamese MiGs, in two raids, off the coast of North Vietnam. They were repulsed by missiles and gunfire, with no damage incurred by the Biddle. One MiG was destroyed by a Terrier missile, with a second possibly destroyed.

20th Lynne Cox, a 15-year-old girl, set a new record for swimming the English Channel, becoming the first person to make the crossing from England to France in less than ten hours. Her record of 9 hours and 57 minutes would be broken later in the year by Richard Hart, whose record she would break the following years.

26th The lucrative contract for construction of the American space shuttle orbiter was awarded to North American Rockwell Corporation.

31st Delta Airlines Flight 841 from Detroit was hijacked by five members of the Black Liberation Army as it was approaching Miami. After receiving $1,000,000 ransom, the 86 hostage/passengers were released and the hijackers commandeered the plane to Boston, and then flew 5,000 miles to Algeria. Four of the hijackers were captured and convicted in 1976, while the elusive fifth, George Wright (who identified himself on the passenger manifest as "Rev. L. Burgess") was on the run for the next 39 years. Wright was finally found and arrested in Lisbon, Portugal, on 26th September 2011.

August

2nd At Benghazi, Egypt's President Anwar Sadat and Libya's leader, Muammar al-Gaddafi, announced that their two countries would unite into one nation by the 1st September 1973. "The Arabs have realized that the challenges of Zionism and imperialism can only be surmounted by a large entity with enormous resources and capabilities", an Egyptian press release stated. The Egypt–Libya union, which never took place, would have had the ninth largest area in the world, at 1,066,407 mi2 (2,761,991 km2).

6th A baseball game was "called on account of grasshoppers" when millions of the insects swarmed into Hogan Park at Midland, Texas, during the second game of a doubleheader. In the Texas League game, the Amarillo Giants had beaten the Midland Cubs 5–4 in the first game. As Amarillo began the second game, grasshoppers dimmed the lighting and alighted upon many of the 857 spectators. Midland won 2–1 when the game was made up the next day.

August

10th | A meteor came within 58 km (36 mi) of the Earth, entering the atmosphere over Utah at 20:28:29 GMT and departing 101 seconds later at 20:30:10 over Canada, before skipping back out. The fireball was visible in daylight, with the occurrence happening at 2:28 pm local time.

11th | With the deactivation of the 3rd Battalion of the 21st U.S. Infantry, the last American ground combat units were pulled out of South Vietnam. The 1,043 man unit had been assigned to the U.S. airbase at Da Nang. Air and sea operations continued and more than 40,000 U.S. servicemen remained in Vietnam.

14th | In the worst aviation accident in Germany to date, all 156 people on board an Ilyushin Il-62 of East German Interflug were killed when the aircraft crashed near Königs Wusterhausen.

18th | A "hotline" between South Korea and North Korea was established, as telephone links between Seoul and Pyongyang were reopened for the first time since the 1950 outbreak of the Korean War.

19th | The first daytime episode of the second incarnation of American game show The Price Is Right was taped at CBS Television City, to be aired on 4th September 1972.

26th | The 1972 Summer Olympics opened in Munich, West Germany, with the parade starting at 3:00 local time, and were declared open at 4:25 in the afternoon. The games featured 8,005 athletes from 122 nations. Gunter Zahn lit the torch.

29th | President Nixon announced that 12,000 more American soldiers would be withdrawn from Vietnam over a three-month period, with only 27,000 remaining by 1st December. The withdrawal would represent a 95% drop since the peak of 543,400 in April 1969.

31st | At the Olympics, American sprinters Eddie Hart, Rey Robinson and Robert Taylor were scheduled to run in the quarterfinals of the 100 meter dash, which their coach, Stan Wright, said would take place at 7:00 pm. Shortly before 4:15, the three men were watching a television feed to ABC Sports, and realized that the quarterfinal heats were taking place at that moment. Hart and Robinson arrived too late, and Taylor arrived in time to run his heat without preparation. Coach Wright took the blame for the mix-up, which happened when he relied on a 1971 schedule.

September

4th | Mark Spitz became the first competitor to win seven medals at a single Olympic Games, swimming as part of the American team in the 400 meter relay.

5th | What would end as the Munich massacre began at the 1972 Summer Olympics were in progress, eight members of the Palestinian terrorist group Black September broke into the Olympic Village in Munich, killed two members of Israel's Olympic team, and took nine others hostage. A rescue attempt the next day would end in disaster.

6th | The Munich massacre took place following a bungled attempt by West Germany police to rescue kidnapped members of the Israeli Olympic team, held at Fürstenfeldbruck airport; Palestinian gunmen murdered all nine of their hostages. Five of the terrorists and one policeman died. The Olympic games resumed after a brief interruption.

September

8th | In retaliation for the killing of nine Israeli Olympic athletes in the Munich massacre, Israel's air force bombed Palestinian strongholds in Syria and Lebanon.

9th | At the 1972 Summer Olympics in Munich, the American men's basketball team, which had 64 victories and no defeats since the sport was added in 1936, lost to the Soviet Union, 51–50, on a shot at the buzzer by Alexander Belov. The U.S. team had been ahead, 50–49, when time first ran out, but Olympic officials added three seconds to the clock. The Soviets won the gold medal, and the Americans voted unanimously to refuse the silver medal.

10th | Brazilian driver Emerson Fittipaldi won the Italian Grand Prix at Monza and became, at age 25, the youngest Formula One world champion.

12th | The attack on two British fishing trawlers, by the Icelandic gunboat ICGV Aegir, triggered the second Cod War between the UK and Iceland.

14th | More than 33 years after the outbreak of World War II, West Germany and Poland restored diplomatic relations. East Germany had been an ally of Poland since that nation's establishment in 1949.

17th | The television series M*A*S*H began an eleven-season run, eight years longer than the Korean War which provided its setting.

19th | A parcel bomb sent to the Israeli Embassy in London killed Ami Schachori, the agricultural attaché, who was scheduled to return home after four years abroad. Another bomb arrived at the Israeli Embassy in Paris later in the day, but was disarmed. Both packages had been sent from Amsterdam. Other packages were delivered the next day in New York and Montreal, and defused.

20th | Floyd Patterson's comeback attempt came to an end with a bout against Muhammad Ali. Patterson, the world heavyweight boxing champion from 1956 to 1959, and 1961 to 1962, had been attempting to regain his crown since 1970. The fight was stopped in the seventh round after Ali opened a cut over Patterson's eye.

25th | Voters in Norway decided whether to approve Norway's entry into the Common Market; voters rejected the Treaty of Accession. The final vote was 1,118,281 "Nei" and 971,687 "Ja". On 28th November 1994, voters rejected a second proposal to join the European Community.

27th | Canada banned the sale and use of firecrackers.

October

1st | Publication of the first reports of the production of a recombinant DNA molecule marked the birth of modern molecular biology methodology.

3rd | The Anti-Ballistic Missile Treaty went into effect following ratification by both the United States and the Soviet Union, as did the Interim Agreement on Offensive Forces.

5th | In New York, the General Agreement on Participation was signed between the governments of oil exporters Saudi Arabia, Kuwait, Qatar and the United Arab Emirates on one side, and representatives of the petroleum producing corporations Exxon, Chevron, Texaco and Mobil. In return for a total of $500,000,000 a 25% interest in the Arab-American Company, Aramco, was sold by the oil companies to the four OPEC nations, with an objective of the national oil companies of each country acquiring a 51% ownership by 1983.

8th | In a nationally televised baseball game of the American League championship series, shortstop Bert Campaneris of the Oakland A's hurled his bat at pitcher Lerrin La Grow, after being struck by a wild pitch. "Campy" was barred from further postseason play and fined $500.

12th | A brawl on board the aircraft carrier U.S.S. Kitty Hawk injured 46 people. About 100 black and white sailors fought for hours with knives, forks and chains, before the fight was broken up by a squad of U.S. Marines. Details were released six weeks afterward by the U.S. Navy. The fight began when a sailor asked for two sandwiches at the ship's mess hall and was given only one. Twenty-five men, all black, were charged.

14th | A TV western with a Buddhist theme, Kung Fu premiered as a television series on the American ABC network and ran for three seasons.

16th | Direct deposit by electronic funds transfer made its debut, as a service of several California banks.

18th | The Soviet Union agreed to pay the United States $722,000,000 over a period of 30 years as repayment for American assistance made to the Soviets during World War II under the Lend-Lease Act.

19th | With the beginning of a three-day Paris summit meeting, the leaders of the nine members of the recently enlarged European Community came together for the first time.

23rd | The United States halted bombing of North Vietnam above the 20th parallel, bringing to a close Operation Linebacker after nearly six months.

25th | In its continuing investigation of the Watergate scandal, the Washington Post reported that White House Chief of Staff H. R. Haldeman was the fifth person to control a secret cash fund designed to finance illegal political sabotage and espionage during the 1972 presidential election campaign.

27th | Mariner 9 was switched off after having transmitted 7,329 images since its arrival into orbit (13th November 1971) over the planet Mars.

28th | The Airbus A300, first airliner built by the Airbus company, flew for the first time, in France.

30th | Don Rogers was signed by Crystal Palace FC, which paid Swindon Town £147,000 for his services. He would go on to play 83 games for Palace scoring 30 goals, including two in a 5-0 rout of Manchester United on 16th December.

November

1st The ground breaking, made-for-television film That Certain Summer appeared as the ABC Wednesday Night Movie. Actors Hal Holbrook and Martin Sheen addressed a controversial topic, portraying an adult gay couple in the Golden Globe winning movie.

3rd A group of 132 sailors on board the USS Constellation, mostly African-American, began what has been described as "the first mass mutiny in the history of the U.S. Navy". The men refused to leave the mess deck in protest over announcements, the day before, that 250 black sailors would be discharged, six of them less than honourably, and demanded to meet with ship Captain J.D. Ward. The next day, the men disobeyed a direct order to report to the flight deck, and on November 9, the men refused orders to return to the ship while in San Diego. None of the sailors were ever arrested. Some were discharged early, and most were reassigned to shore duty.

5th Organic farming entered a new era when the International Federation of Organic Agriculture Movements (IFOAM) was founded in Versailles, France, by five organizations from France, Great Britain, Sweden, South Africa and the United States.

6th A fire broke out in the dining car of an express train in Japan while it was traveling through an eight-mile long tunnel near Fukui. The smoke killed 29 people and injured another 678.

8th HBO (Home Box Office), the first "pay cable" television channel, was launched in the United States at 7:30 pm ET. The first evening of programming was a National Hockey League (NHL) game between the New York Rangers and the Vancouver Canucks from Madison Square Garden (part of a long-term agreement to broadcast sports events based at the Manhattan arena), followed by the film Sometimes a Great Notion, and was broadcast to 365 subscribers in Wilkes-Barre, Pennsylvania. Each household paid an additional $6.00 per month to Service Electric Cable TV for the service.

9th Canada's first geostationary communications satellite, Anik-1 was launched from Florida. The project was a joint venture by Telesat Canada and the Hughes Aircraft Company.

14th The Dow Jones Industrial Average closed above 1,000 (at 1,003.16) for the first time in its history. The Dow had fluctuated above 1,000 five other times, but had never finished the day at four figures.

16th The Pepsi Cola Company announced a deal with Soyuzplodimport for Pepsi to be bottled and sold in the Soviet Union, making the drink the first American cola (and consumer product) to be made in the U.S.S.R.

November

18th	The USS Sanctuary became the first U.S. Navy ship to transport women sailors assigned to sea duty, with 40 enlisted women and 30 nurses assigned to work with the 480 men. The recommissioning of the ship was carried out as "part of a pilot program to evaluate the utilization of women for shipboard duty."
21st	In Epping, British daredevil Stephen Ladd successfully rode his motorcycle through a 50-yard-long tunnel of fire created by blazing bales of hay, but then persuaded organizers to let him try again as the flames got fiercer. On his second run, Ladd's motorcycle failed inside the tunnel, and he died of his burns.
22nd	An American Boeing B-52 Stratofortress was shot down, the first to be downed by enemy fire in the Vietnam War.
27th	In the first episode of the fourth season of Sesame Street, the character of "The Count" (officially Count von Count) was introduced. True to his name, the friendly children's show puppet vampire (performed by Jerry Nelson) helped children count.
29th	Atari, Inc. released the seminal arcade version of Pong, the first such game to achieve commercial success.
30th	As the "Cod War" between fishing trawlers in the North Atlantic Ocean escalated, the British Foreign Secretary, Sir Alec Douglas-Home announced that Royal Navy ships would be stationed to protect British trawlers off the coast of Iceland.

December

1st	India and Pakistan exchanged prisoners of war taken during the 1971 war between the two nations. In all, 542 Pakistanis and 639 Indians were repatriated.
2nd	One of the most spectacular examples of a sinkhole was formed in a matter of hours in Shelby County, Alabama. The "December Giant", also known as the "Golly Hole" sank to a depth of 150 feet and left a 450-by-350-foot-wide (140 by 110 m) crater.
5th	Screening of all passengers and carry-on luggage would be required in all American airports by 5th January 1973, under emergency regulations announced the United States Department of Transportation. Federal funds would pay for the equipment, and the additional personnel would be paid for by the airlines and airport operators. There had been 29 hijackings in the United States in 1972. In 1973 there were two.
7th	Apollo 17 was launched from Cape Kennedy at 12:33 a.m. EST after a delay of nearly three hours. Carrying astronauts Gene Cernan, Ronald Evans, and Harrison Schmitt, the mission was the last manned trip to the Moon. With an orbital trajectory that permitted a fully illuminated view of the entire planet, the crew snapped a famous image of the globe, colloquially called "The Blue Marble" After three hours, rockets were fired and the three astronauts of Apollo 17 became the last persons to go beyond the orbit of the Earth.
9th	Pilot Martin Hartwell was rescued in the Canadian Arctic more than a month after he and three other persons had crashed near Great Bear Lake in the Northwest Territories. The plane's disappearance had led to the largest aviation search in Canada's history.
11th	Mankind landed on the Moon for the sixth and last time, as the Apollo 17 lunar module Challenger touched down at 1955 GMT at the Taurus-Litrow crater at 1:54 pm Houston time (1954 GMT).

December

13th North Vietnam's negotiators walked out of the Paris Peace Talks. President Nixon issued an ultimatum to the North Vietnamese to return to the talks within 72 hours, or face severe measures. On 18th December the United States began Operation Linebacker II, the most massive aerial bombardment ever made of North Vietnam.

14th Shortly after midnight Eastern Standard Time, American astronaut Eugene Cernan climbed into the lunar module Challenger, following after Harrison Schmitt, having been the last person to have set foot on the moon; the scheduled end of the moonwalk had been 0433 GMT (11:33 pm 13th December EST). At 2255 GMT (5:55 pm EST), the cabin of the Challenger lunar module lifted off from the surface of the Moon with Cernan and Schmitt, to return to lunar orbit.

18th Neilia Hunter Biden, the wife of U.S. Senator-elect (and future U.S. Vice-President and President-elect) Joe Biden was killed in a traffic accident, along with the couple's 13-month-old daughter, Naomi. Mrs. Biden's car was struck by a tractor-trailer at 2:30 pm as she pulled into an intersection near Hockessin, Delaware. The Biden's' two sons, aged three and four, were injured.

19th The supertanker Sea Star collided with another ship and spilled 144,000,000 litres of petroleum into the Persian Gulf.

24th U.S. bombing of North Vietnam was temporarily halted for 36 hours at 8:00 am local time on Christmas Eve, although Radio Hanoi reported that raids had continued as late as 7:30 pm.

25th An unpublished decree took effect in the U.S.S.R., making it illegal for Soviet residents to meet with foreigners "for the purpose of disseminating false or slanderous information about the Soviet Union", a definition that covered most dissidents.

27th The Environmental Protection Agency issued new regulations requiring unleaded gasoline to be available in all American stations no later than the 1st July 1974, with a limit 0.05 grams of lead per gallon.

30th The "Christmas Bombing" of North Vietnam halted by order of U.S. President Nixon, after the North Vietnamese agreed to resume negotiations with Henry Kissinger beginning on 8th January. A total of 20,370 tons of bombs were dropped on North Vietnam over eleven days.

PEOPLE IN POWER

Gough Whitlam
1972-1975
Australia
Prime Minister

Georges Pompidou
1969-1974
France
Président

Emílio Garrastazu Médici
1969-1974
Brazil
President

Pierre Elliott Trudeau
1968-1979
Canada
Prime Minister

Mao Zedong
1943-1976
China
Government of China

Willy Brandt
1969-1974
Germany
President of Germany

Varahagiri Venkata Giri
1969-1974
India
4th President of India

Giovanni Leone
1971-1978
Italy
President

Hiroito
1926-1989
Japan
Emperor

Luis Echeverría
1970-1976
Mexico
President of Mexico

Leonid Brezhnev
1964-1982
Russia
Premier

Jacobus Johannes Fouché
1968-1975
South Africa
Prime Minister

Richard Nixon
1969-1974
United States
President

Gaston Eyskens
1968-1973
Belgium
Prime Minister

Keith Holyoake
1960-1972
New Zealand
Prime Minister

Sir Edward Heath
1970-1974
United Kingdom
Prime Minister

Olof Palme
1969-1976
Sweden
Prime Minister

Anker Jørgensen
1972-1973
Denmark
Prime Minister

Francisco Franco
1936-1975
Spain
President

János Kádár
1956-1988
Hungary
Hungarian Working
People's Party

The Year You Were Born 1972
Book by Sapphire Publishing
© All rights reserved

Printed in Great Britain
by Amazon

78970324R00047